# Bud, Not Buddy

## with Connections

**Also by Christopher Paul Curtis in HRW Library:**

*The Watsons Go to Birmingham—1963*

# Bud, Not Buddy

Christopher Paul Curtis

## with
## Connections

**HOLT, RINEHART AND WINSTON**

A Harcourt Classroom Education Company

**Austin** · New York · Orlando · Atlanta · San Francisco · Boston · Dallas · Toronto · London

For permission to reprint copyrighted material, grateful acknowledgment is made to the following sources:

**Delacorte Press, an imprint of Random House Children's Books, a division of Random House, Inc., New York, New York.:** *Bud, Not Buddy* by Christopher Paul Curtis. Copyright © 1999 by Christopher Paul Curtis. All rights reserved.

**Steve Boerner:** From "Biography: 1761–1765" by Steve Boerner from *The Mozart Project,* accessed November 15, 2000 at http://www.frontiernet.net/~sboerner/mozart/biography/ bi_61_65.html#2. Copyright © 2000 by Steve Boerner. **Civitas Press, a member of Perseus Books L.L.C.:** From "The Life of A. Philip Randolph" from *Africana* by Kwame Appiah and Henry Louis Gates. Copyright © 2000 by Afropaedia, LLC. **The Detroit News:** From "How the Great Depression Changed Detroit" by Jenny Nolan from *Rearview Mirror: A Living History Project* from the Story and Photo Archives of *The Detroit News,* accessed November 15, 2000 at http://www.detnews.com/history/depress/depress.htm. Copyright © 2000 by The Detroit News. **HarperCollins Publishers, Inc.:** From *Black Boy* by Richard Wright. Copyright 1937, 1942, 1944, 1945 by Richard Wright; copyright renewed © 1973 by Ellen Wright. **Scholastic Inc.:** "An Hour with Abuelo" from *An Island Like You: Stories of the Barrio* by Judith Ortiz Cofer. Copyright © 1995 by Judith Ortiz Cofer. Published by Orchard Books, an imprint of Scholastic Inc.

Cover art: John Hull

**I dedicate this book to the following people:**

*Leslie and Herman Curtis Jr.,*
*Sarah and Earl Lewis,*
*Hazel and Herman E. Curtis Sr.,*
*Joan and George Taylor,*
*Nina and Sterling Sleet,*
*Gloria and Frederick "Bud" Curtis,*
*Virginia and F. D. Johnson,*
*Paul Lewis,*
*Donna and Eugene Miller,*
*Johnnie and Don Ricks,*
*Rosemary and Willie Swan,*
*Laverne and James Cross Sr.,*
*Carolyn and Dan Evans,*
*Willie Frances and Robert James,*
*Dorothy and Theodore Johnson,*
*Tommie and Robert Epps Sr.,*
*Mr. and Mrs. Small of Liberty Street,*
*James Wesley Sr.,*
*Harrison Edward Patrick,*
*James Cross Jr.,*
*LaRon Williams, Douglas Tennant,*
*Margaret Davidson,*
*Roland Alums,*
*John Nash,*
*Suzanne Henry Jakeway*
*and Alvin Stockard—*

*all of whom led and lead by example, all of whom have been*
*models of compassion, strength and love, all of whom*
*I'll remember forever.*

# Acknowledgements

I am so fortunate to have been welcomed into the world of literature for young people, I want to give heartfelt thanks to everyone at Delacorte Press for all they have done to make this experience so memorable, especially Mary Raymond, Andrew Smith, Terry Borzumato, Melissa Kazan and Craig Virden. Thank you to my agent extraordinaire, Charlotte Sheedy, and Neeti Madan and David Forrer; to the people who preread *Bud, Not Buddy,* for their insights: Paulette Bracy, Joanne Portalupi, Joan Kettle, Manjuli Kodagoda, Ashly Flannery, Melanie Morrison, Jordan MacNevin and Rose Matte; and to the many teachers and librarians I've met who are on the front lines every day, giving so much of themselves to young people, among them John Jarvey, Ray Kettle, Terry Fisher, Janet Brown, Jean Brown, Elaine Stephens, Teresa Jindo, Kylene Beers and Teri Lesesne. What an unheralded, beautiful job these people do.

I also wish to thank a group of authors who have generously given encouragement at every opportunity: Jacqueline Woodson, Ralph Fletcher, James Ransome, Arnold Adoff, Graham Salisbury, Jerry Spinelli, Ashley Bryan and Robert Cormier; and special thanks to two writers who have no idea how important their shoulders and words have been to me: Paula Danziger and Chris Crutcher.

There is also a group of people whose friendship, support and encouragement are such an integral part of my life that there is no need to mention them. However, to avoid any unpleasant scenes, dirty looks and general disruption of my home life, I know I've got to do it anyway: Special thanks to Steven Curtis, Cydney McKenzie Curtis, Leslie Curtis, Cydney Eleanor Curtis, Joan Taylor, Lynn Guest, Maureen Flannery, Celestine Crayton, Kathleen Small and Liz Ivette Torres.

My gratitude as well to Flint's Betty Carter, the musical inspiration for Miss Thomas.

Finally, eternal thanks to the two people who have contributed the most to my writing: my editor, Wendy Lamb, who has been kind enough never to say "I told you so," and my rock, my wife, Kaysandra Sookram Curtis.

# Contents

# Bud, Not Buddy

# CHAPTER 1

*HERE WE GO AGAIN.* We were all standing in line waiting for breakfast when one of the caseworkers came in and *tap-tap-tap*ped down the line. Uh-oh, this meant bad news, either they'd found a foster home for somebody or somebody was about to get paddled. All the kids watched the woman as she moved along the line, her high-heeled shoes sounding like little firecrackers going off on the wooden floor.

Shoot! She stopped at me and said, "Are you Buddy Caldwell?"

I said, "It's Bud, not Buddy, ma'am."

She put her hand on my shoulder and took me out of line. Then she pulled Jerry, one of the littler boys, over. "Aren't you Jerry Clark?" He nodded.

"Boys, good news! Now that the school year has ended, you both have been accepted in new temporary-care homes starting this afternoon!"

Jerry asked the same thing I was thinking. "Together?"

She said, "Why, no. Jerry, you'll be in a family with three little girls . . ."

Jerry looked like he'd just found out they were going to dip him in a pot of boiling milk.

". . . and Bud . . ." She looked at some papers she was holding. "Oh, yes, the Amoses, you'll be with Mr. and Mrs. Amos and their son, who's twelve years old, that makes him just two years older than you, doesn't it, Bud?"

"Yes, ma'am."

She said, "I'm sure you'll both be very happy."

Me and Jerry looked at each other.

The woman said, "Now, now, boys, no need to look so glum. I know you don't understand what it means, but there's a depression going on all over this country. People can't find jobs and these are very, very difficult times for everybody. We've been lucky enough to find two wonderful families who've opened their doors for you. I think it's best that we show our new foster families that we're very . . ."

She dragged out the word *very,* waiting for us to finish her sentence for her.

Jerry said, "Cheerful, helpful and grateful." I moved my lips and mumbled.

She smiled and said, "Unfortunately, you won't have time for breakfast. I'll have a couple of pieces of fruit put in a bag. In the meantime go to the sleep room and strip your beds and gather all of your things."

Here we go again. I felt like I was walking in my sleep as I followed Jerry back to the room where all the boys' beds were jim-jammed together. This was the third foster home I was going to and I'm used to packing up and leaving, but it still surprises me that there are always a few seconds, right after they tell you you've got to go, when my nose gets all runny and my throat gets all choky and my eyes get all sting-y. But the tears coming out doesn't happen to me anymore, I don't know when it first happened, but it seems like my eyes don't cry no more.

Jerry sat on his bed and I could tell that he was losing the fight not to cry. Tears were popping out of his eyes and slipping down his cheeks.

I sat down next to him and said, "I know being in a house with three girls sounds terrible, Jerry, but it's a lot better than being with a boy who's a couple of years older than you. I'm the one who's going to have problems. A older boy is going to want to fight, but those little girls are going to treat you real good. They're going to treat you like some kind of special pet or something."

Jerry said, "You really think so?"

I said, "I'd trade you in a minute. The worst thing that's going to happen to you is that they're going to make you play house a lot. They'll probably make you be the baby and will hug you and do this kind of junk to you." I tickled Jerry under his chin and said, "Ga-ga goo-goo, baby-waby."

Jerry couldn't help but smile. I said, "You're going to be great."

Jerry looked like he wasn't so scared anymore so I went over to my bed and started getting ready.

Even though it was me who was in a lot of trouble I couldn't help but feel sorry for Jerry. Not only because he was going to have to live around three girls, but also because being six is a real rough age to be at. Most folks think you start to be a real adult when you're fifteen or sixteen years old, but that's not true, it really starts when you're around six.

It's at six that grown folks don't think you're a cute little kid anymore, they talk to you and expect that you understand everything they mean. And you'd best understand too, if you aren't looking for some real trouble, 'cause it's around six that grown folks stop giving you little swats and taps and jump clean up to giving you slugs that'll knock you right down and have you seeing stars in the middle of the day. The first foster home I was in taught me that real quick.

Six is a bad time too 'cause that's when some real scary things start to happen to your body, it's around then that your teeth start coming a-loose in your mouth.

You wake up one morning and it seems like your tongue is the first one to notice that something strange is going on, 'cause as soon as you get up there it is pushing and rubbing up against one of your front teeth and I'll be doggoned if that tooth isn't the littlest bit wiggly.

At first you think it's kind of funny, but the tooth keeps getting looser and looser and one day, in the middle of pushing the tooth back and forth and squinching your eyes shut, you pull it clean out. It's the scariest thing you can think of 'cause you lose control of your tongue at the same time and no matter how hard you try to stop it, it won't leave the new hole in your mouth alone, it keeps digging around in the spot where that tooth used to be.

You tell some adult about what's happening but all they do is say it's normal. You can't be too sure, though, 'cause it shakes you up a whole lot more than grown folks think it does when perfectly good parts of your body commence to loosening up and falling off of you.

Unless you're as stupid as a lamppost you've got to wonder what's coming off next, your arm? Your leg? Your neck? Every morning when you wake up it seems a lot of your parts aren't stuck on as good as they used to be.

Six is real tough. That's how old I was when I came to live here in the Home. That's how old I was when Momma died.

I folded the blanket and sheet and set them back on the mattress. Then I reached under the bed to get my suitcase. Most of the kids in the Home keep their things in a paper or cloth sack, but not me. I have my own suitcase.

I set it on the mattress and untied the twine that held it together. I did what I do every night before I go to sleep, I checked to make sure everything was there. The way there're more and more kids coming into the Home every day, I had to make sure no one had run off with any of my things.

First I pulled my blanket out and saw that everything was where it was supposed to be. At the bottom of my suitcase were the flyers. I took the blue flyer out and looked at it again.

The paper was starting to wear out from me looking at it so much but I liked checking to see if there was anything I hadn't noticed before. It was like something was telling me there was a message for me on this flyer but I didn't have the decoder ring to read what it was.

Across the top of the flyer writ in big black letters were the words LIMITED ENGAGEMENT, then in little letters it said, "Direct from an S.R.O. engagement in New York City." Underneath that in big letters again it said,

"HERMAN E. CALLOWAY and the Dusky Devastators of the Depression!!!!!!"

Those six exclamation points made it seem like this was the most important news anyone could think of, seems like you'd have to be really great to deserve all of those exclamation points all stacked up in a row like that.

Next the paper said, "Masters of the New Jazz," then in the middle of the flyer was a blurry picture of the man I have a real good suspicion about. I've never met him, but I have a pretty good feeling that this guy must be my father.

In the picture he's standing next to a giant fiddle that's taller than him. It looks like it's real heavy 'cause he's leaning up against it trying to hold it up. He looks like he's been doing this for a long time and he must be tired 'cause he has a droopy, dreamy look on his face. There are two men beside him, one playing drums and the other one blowing a horn.

It wasn't hard to see what the guy who must be my father was like just by looking at his picture. You could tell he was a real quiet, real friendly and smart man, he had one of those kind of faces. Underneath the picture someone had writ with a black fountain pen, "One Night Only in Flint, Michigan, at the Luxurious Fifty Grand on Saturday June 16, 1932. 9 Until ?"

I remember Momma bringing this flyer with her when she came from working one day, I remember because she got very upset when she put it on the supper table and kept looking at it and picking it up and putting it back and moving it around. I was only six then and couldn't understand why this one got her so upset, she kept four others that were a lot like it in her dressing table, but this one really got her jumpy. The only difference I could see between the blue one and the others was that the others didn't say anything about Flint on them.

I remember this blue one too 'cause it wasn't too long after she brought it home that I knocked on Momma's bedroom door, then found her.

I put the blue flyer back in the suitcase with the four older ones and put everything back in its place.

I went over to the big chest of drawers and took my other set of clothes out and put them in the suitcase too. I tied the twine back around my bag, then went and sat on Jerry's bed with him. Jerry must've been thinking just as hard as I was 'cause neither one of us said nothing, we just sat close enough so that our shoulders were touching.

Here we go again.

# CHAPTER 2

*THERE COMES A TIME* when you're losing a fight that it just doesn't make sense to keep on fighting. It's not that you're being a quitter, it's just that you've got the sense to know when enough is enough.

I was having this thought because Todd Amos was hitting me so hard and fast that I knew that the blood squirting out of my nose was only the beginning of a whole long list of bad things that were about to happen to me.

Todd's next punch crashed into the side of my ear and

I fell on the floor and pulled my knees up to my chest and crossed my arms in front of my head like a turtle in a shell. I started scooching toward the bed hoping I could get under it.

Todd started kicking me but his slippers couldn't hurt me near as much as his fists had. The bedroom door opened and his mother, Mrs. Amos, came in. It seemed like she was having a hard time figuring out what was going on because Todd's right leg got tired from kicking me and he switched over to his left one while she watched.

Finally Mrs. Amos said kind of soft, "Toddy?"

Todd looked up, fell on his knees and put his hands on his throat. He started huffing and puffing with his eyes bucking out of his head and his chest going up and down so hard that it looked like some kind of big animal was inside of him trying to bust out. This was my chance to get under the bed and pull the covers down so they couldn't see me.

Mrs. Amos ran over to her son and fell on her knees. She put her arms around his shoulders.

"Toddy? Toddy boy, are you all right?" She looked over to where I was peeking from under the bed. "You little cur, what have you done to Toddy?"

Todd coughed out, "Oh, Mother . . ." He took in two jumbo breaths. "I was only trying to help . . ."—he was sounding like a horse that had been run too hard in the winter—"and . . . and look what it's gotten me."

Todd pointed at his jaw and Mrs. Amos and me could both see a perfect print in the shape of my hand welted up on Todd's blubbery cheek.

With one quick snatch she had me from under the bed and out on the floor laying down next to Todd.

"How dare you! This is how you choose to repay me? Not only have you struck him, you have provoked his asthma!"

Todd said, "I just tried to waken him to make sure he'd gone to the lavatory, Mother. I was just trying to help." He aimed his finger dead at me and said, "And look at him, Mother, this one's got 'bed wetter' written all over him."

I'm not bragging when I say that I'm one of the best liars in the world but I got to tell you, Todd was pretty doggone good. It seemed like he knew some of the same things I know, the things I think of all the time and try to remember so I don't make the same mistake more than seven or eight times. Shucks, I've got so many of them rememorized that I had to give them numbers, and it seemed like Todd knew Number 3 of Bud Caldwell's Rules and Things for Having a Funner Life and Making a Better Liar Out of Yourself.

### RULES AND THINGS NUMBER 3

**If You Got to Tell a Lie, Make Sure
It's Simple and Easy to Remember.**

Todd had done that. But this wasn't really a good test because Mrs. Amos had her ears set to believe anything Todd said. In her eyes Todd's mouth was a prayer book.

But I can't blame Todd for lying like that, having someone who likes you so much that they think everything you say is the truth has got to be a liar's paradise, that might feel so good it could make you want to quit lying. But maybe not, 'cause Todd hadn't quit lying since the second I came to his house.

What had really happened was that I woke up from a good sleep because it felt like a steam locomotive had jumped the tracks and chug-chug-chugged its way straight into my nose.

When I'd jerked up in bed and opened my eyes Todd was standing next to me with a yellow pencil in his hand. He was looking at it like it was a thermometer and said, "Wow! You got all the way up to *R*!"

He turned the pencil toward me, crunched up against the headboard. I saw TICONDEROGA printed on the yellow wood.

The whole room smelled like the rubber from the eraser and I was winking and blinking my left eye because it felt like something had poked the back of my eyeball.

Todd laughed. "I've never gotten it in as deep as the *N* on any of you other little street urchins. I just might enjoy your stay here. Who knows what other things you could be number one in, Buddy?"

I'd already told him twice that my name was Bud, not Buddy.

I didn't care that Todd Amos was twelve years old, I didn't care that he was twice as big as me, and I didn't care that his mother was being paid to take care of me. I wasn't about to let anybody call me Buddy and stick a pencil up my nose all the way to the *R*.

I swung as hard as I could at Todd's big balloon head.

Somewhere between the time I threw my punch and the time it landed my fist came open and when my hand landed it made a pop like a .22 rifle going off. Todd fell on the floor like he'd been coldcocked.

He sputtered and muttered and felt the spot where I'd slapped him. Then a big smile came on his face and he stood up and started walking real slow toward where I was on the bed. He untied his robe and dropped it on the floor like he was getting ready to do some hard work.

I jumped to the floor and got my fists up. Todd might've been a lot bigger than me but he'd better be ready, this wasn't going to be a bird's nest sitting on the ground for him. He could kiss my wrist if he thought I was going to let him whip me up without a good fight.

Being this brave was kind of stupid. Even though Todd was a puffy, rich old mama's boy who wore a robe and slippers he could hit like a mule and it wasn't too long before I'd decided enough was enough.

But the story that Mrs. Amos was hearing from her

lying son was only that Todd had tried to wake me up so I could go to the bathroom.

Mrs. Amos hated bed wetters more than anything in the world and my bed had a sticky, hot, smelly rubber baby sheet on it. She'd said it wasn't anything personal and after I had proved myself for two or three months I could get a proper cloth sheet, but until then she had to protect her mattress.

She pulled Todd to his feet and led him to the door. She looked over at me. "You are a beastly little brute and I will not tolerate even one night with you under my roof. Who knows what you would be capable of while we slept?"

The door shut behind them and I heard a key jiggle in the lock.

I plugged the right side of my nose and tried real hard to blow the smell of rubber out of the left side.

The key jiggled in the lock again. This time when the door opened Mr. Amos was standing with Mrs. Amos. He was carrying my suitcase. Uh-oh, they'd looked inside. I could tell because the twine that held it together was tied in a kind of knot that I didn't know.

This was wrong. They'd promised they'd keep it safe and not look in it. They'd laughed at me when I made them promise, but they did promise.

"Boy," Mrs. Amos said, "I am not the least bit surprised at your show of ingratitude. Lord knows I have been stung by my own people before. But take a good look at me because I am one person who is totally fed up with you and your ilk. I do not have time to put up with the foolishness of those members of our race who do not want to be uplifted. In the morning I'll be getting in touch with the Home and, much as a bad penny, you shall be returning to them. I am a woman of my word, though, and you shall not spend one night in my house."

She looked at her husband. "Mr. Amos will show you to the shed tonight and you can come back in tomorrow for breakfast before you go. I do hope your conscience plagues you because you may have ruined things for many others. I do not know if I shall ever be able to help another child in need. I do know I shall not allow vermin to attack my poor baby in his own house."

She talked like this and she wasn't even a preacher or a teacher. Shucks, she talked strange like this and she wasn't even a librarian.

I only halfway listened to what Mrs. Amos was saying, I was too busy keeping my eye on my suitcase wondering if they'd stolen anything from it. And thinking about getting even.

When I thought she was done talking I reached my hand out for my suitcase but she told Mr. Amos, "Oh, no, we shall hold on to his beloved valuables." She laughed. "This shall be our assurance that nothing comes up missing from the house and that this little animal is still here in the morning. He is far too attached to those treasures to go anywhere without them."

Mrs. Amos was one of those grown-ups who could always think of one more thing to say. "And that is not all. Before you retire to the shed you shall go to Todd and apologize or I shall be forced to give you the strapping of your life."

I'd been so worried about my suitcase that I didn't even notice the thick black razor strap hanging out of Mrs. Amos's hand.

She didn't have to worry, I'd apologize. One beating from these Amoses was enough for me.

She grabbed my arm. Mr. Amos walked out of the room with my suitcase, and Mrs. Amos pulled me down the hall to Todd's room. We stood outside the door listening to Todd groan. When Mr. Amos came back, my suitcase was gone. He'd been so quick that I knew my bag couldn't be too far away.

She tapped on Todd's door and said, "Toddy, may we come in?"

Todd's groans got a lot louder. Finally he said, "Yes, Mother"—choke . . . cough—"come in."

We opened the door and as soon as he saw me Todd got a real terrified look on his face. He scooched up to the headboard and wrapped his arms around his head.

Mrs. Amos gave me a shake and said, "Well?"

I put my head down and started shooting apologies

out like John Dillinger shoots out bullets. I aimed at Todd first. "I know it was wrong of me to hit you. I know you were only trying to help and I'm very sorry for what I did."

I looked at Mr. Amos. "And sir, I'm sorry that I got you out of your sleep."

He rolled his eyes like that was enough for him.

Mrs. Amos was going to be the hardest because just like her ears were set to believe everything that came out of Todd's lips they were set not to believe anything I said. And if I didn't lie good enough she was going to use that strap on me. These Amoses might look like a bunch of cream puffs but if she was anything like Todd I bet she could pack a real wallop.

"And Mrs. Amos, I'm so grateful for all of your help. And I'm really, really sorry."

I looked up and could see she needed more. "If you give me another chance I promise I'll do a whole lot better. Please don't call the Home, please don't send me back." Shucks, going back to the Home was just what I wanted to do, but I was being just like Brer Rabbit in one of the books Momma used to read to me at night when he yelled out, "Please, Brer Fox, don't throw me into the pricker patch, please, please!"

This was another one of Bud Caldwell's Rules and Things to Have a Funner Life and Make a Better Liar of Yourself.

## RULES AND THINGS NUMBER 118

**You Have to Give Adults Something That
They Think They Can Use to Hurt You by Taking it
Away. That Way They Might Not Take Something
Away That You Really Do Want. Unless
They're Crazy or Real Stupid They Won't Take
Everything Because if They Did They Wouldn't
Have Anything to Hold Over
Your Head to Hurt You with Later.**

I stopped talking and gave Mrs. Amos a chance to jump right in.

She held her hand up in my face and said, "Enough. Mr. Amos, give him the blanket and pillow off the bed he was in and put him in the shed."

Todd said, "Yeah, Buddy, keep a sharp eye out for the vampire bats in the shed." It was like a miracle, Todd's asthma was gone and he turned into a real chatterbox. "Oh, and watch out for those spiders and centipedes, Buddy. The last kid who got put in there got stung so bad he was swole up as big as a whale when we got him out in the morning."

I guess I didn't look scared enough 'cause Todd kept going. "The kid before that hasn't been found to this day. All that's left is that big puddle of his blood on the floor. Isn't that right, Mother?"

Mrs. Amos said, "Now, Toddy, hush up, you'll just tire yourself out more."

I noticed that she never denied the things Todd had said about the vampires and centipedes and spiders and puddles of blood.

As I followed Mr. Amos I kept a sharp eye out for my suitcase.

When we got to the kitchen the first thing I saw was that there was a double-barreled shotgun leaning against the side of the icebox. I didn't have time to wonder why they'd be so scared they'd keep a big gun like that out in the open because I spotted my suitcase slid way under the kitchen table! I didn't let Mr. Amos know I'd seen it, but it did make me get a lot calmer.

We went out of the back kitchen door and down the steps into the dark.

We walked around to the back of the shed and he put a key in a padlock. A chain rattled, the lock came off and the door creaked open.

Even though it was nighttime there was a whole different, scarier kind of dark in the shed. A colder dark with more grays and more shadows. A old smell leaked out and it seemed like it was the perfect smell that all this gray would have.

Mr. Amos nudged me and I took a baby step into the shed. He could kiss my wrist if he thought I was going to beg him and say things like "I'll do anything you folks ask me if you don't lock me up in here all alone." I squeezed my tongue between my teeth to hold it still 'cause I know a lot of times your brain might want to be brave but your mouth might let some real chicken-sounding stuff fall out of it.

I stood a little bit inside and looked around. Right under the window was a pile of stacked wood. There were a bunch of dusty spiderwebs in front of the little window and someone had pasted old yellow newspapers over the glass so the kids who got locked in here couldn't peek out.

Mr. Amos handed me the blanket and pillow and gave me another nudge. I took two more baby steps in.

I looked down at the floor. If I was like a normal kid I would've busted out crying, but I just stood there breathing hard. It was a good thing I'd bit my tongue, because I came real close to saying those stupid begging words to Mr. Amos. Right in the middle of the floor there was a big black stain in the dirt!

They really were going to make me sleep in a shed with a patch of blood from that kid who had disappeared out of here a couple of weeks ago!

The floor went completely black when Mr. Amos pulled the door shut. I couldn't see it now, but I'd re-memorized the exact shape the stain was in.

The padlock snapped shut with the loudest click I'd ever heard.

# CHAPTER 3

*THE ONLY THING* I could hear was my own breath. It was so loud that it sounded like there were six scared people locked up in the shed.

I closed my eyes and thought real hard about making my breathing slow down. Pretty soon it sounded like the five other breathers in the shed had left. I was still scared but now it was that get-real-excited-and-want-to-move-around kind of scared.

It didn't take too long for my eyes to get used to the dark. There was a gray gas can in one corner next to a bunch of gray rakes and a pile of gray rags, and a gray tire next to some gray fishing poles. Maybe Mr. Amos had only pretended to lock the door.

I reached my hand toward the gray doorknob and quick as that I went from kind of calm to being in that stand-in-one-place-with-spit-drooling-down-the-front-of-your-shirt kind of scared.

Halfway up the door were three little flat monster heads guarding the doorknob. Each head had two little round eyes staring right at me. The eyes were the only thing in the shed that weren't gray. They were a bright yellow with a big black spot right in the middle.

I dropped my blanket and pillow and back-stepped until my legs hit the woodpile behind me. From all the fast breathing going on you'da thought the five other scared people had come back and brought a couple of scared friends with them.

Each head had a wide-open mouth with a sharp set of pointy teeth and lips smiling back ready to bite. It felt like the shed was getting smaller and smaller and the little mouths were getting closer and closer.

Then I knew what I was looking at. The doorknob guards were three dried-out fish heads that someone had nailed to the door.

I ran over to the pile of rags and poked at one of them with my shoe to make sure there weren't any rats or centipedes hiding under it, then I picked it up and hung it over the fish heads so I couldn't see them and they couldn't see me.

I picked up my blanket and pillow and had to decide what was the best way to sleep. I knew the floor was no good, I'da bet all sorts of bugs and roaches were crawling around.

I remember what happened to my best friend, Bugs, when a cockroach crawled in his ear one night at the Home. Four grown folks had held Bugs down whilst they tried to pull it out with a pair of tweezers but the only thing that that did was pull the roach's back legs off. When they were digging around in Bugs's ears with the tweezers you'd've thought they were pulling his legs off, not some cockroach's, I'd never heard a kid scream that loud.

After about fifteen minutes of Bugs screaming the joint down they said they were going to have to take him to the emergency room to get the roach out. It was almost morning when Bugs got back. Everyone was asleep except me.

I waited until they put him in his bed and turned off the lights.

I said, "Did they get it out?"

He said, "Oh, hi, Bud. Yeah, they got him."

"Did it hurt a lot?"

"Nope."

"Were you scared?"

"Nope."

"Then how come you were screaming so doggone loud?"

He said, "I didn't know I was, I probably couldn't hear me screaming 'cause that roach was so loud."

I'd seen lots of roaches but I'd never heard one of them make any sound. I said, "Loud how?"

"Well, bugs ain't so different from us as you'd think, soon as he saw those tweezers coming at him he was pretty terrified and commenced to screaming, screaming in English too, not some bug language like you'd expect from a roach."

"Yeah? What'd he say?"

"All he kept yelling was, 'My legs! My legs! Why have they done this to my legs?' "

That's the true story about how Bugs started getting called Bugs.

I'd bet a thousand dollars that there were roaches on the floor of this shed, just waiting to crawl in someone's ear. And I'd bet those Amoses wouldn't've even tried to pull the roach out, and who knows how long I'd've had to listen to some terrified roach screaming his head off right up against my eardrum?

I spread the blanket on top of the woodpile and climbed up on it. This put me so I was even with the window. I took a piece of bark and brushed all the spiderwebs from in front of the window, then I put my hand on the glass to see if the newspaper was pasted on from the inside or the outside. I touched paper. I spread my fingers and my hand looked like a yellow-jacket bumblebee, bright yellow with black stripes. This was a great place to have shadow puppets so I made my hand be a wolf and a dog and a duck.

After while that got to be pretty boring so I scraped at the paper with my fingernails so I could see outside, but I like to keep my nails bit down real low and the paper didn't budge.

I took out my jackknife and tried scraping the newspaper with it. The paper peeled away in little curly yellow strips like that stuff rich people throw on New Year's Eve. I finally got a hole big enough to look out and mashed my eye up against the glass. I could see the back of the Amos house real clear.

There was a light on. That had to be Mr. and Mrs. Amos's bedroom. The little bit of light that came through the hole in the paper made me get calm enough that I could lay my head on my pillow and take a nap.


WHEN I BLINKED my eyes open, the first thing I noticed was that the light from the Amoses' bedroom was out. The next thing I noticed made me wish I'd stayed asleep.

Up at the very top of the shed was the biggest vampire

bat you'd ever see! He was hanging upside down asleep, but the smell of me rising up to him would probably wake him up at any minute!

I reached over to the window and tried to slide it open. It budged a inch.

I rolled off the woodpile and crawled toward the door with the fish head guards. I reached my hand up and the doorknob turned! Mr. Amos *was* trying to help me! But after the door opened a crack the padlock and chain on the outside held it tight.

I looked back up into the rafters to see if the bat had woke up. He was still sound asleep.

Just like there's a time that a smart person knows enough is enough, there's a time when you know you've got to fight. I wasn't about to let this vampire suck my blood dry without a war, he could kiss my wrist if he thought that was going to happen.

I got up off my knees and picked up the gray rake. I walked over to the woodpile cool as a cucumber. But inside, every part of my guts was shaking.

I stood up on the woodpile and held the rake like it was a Louisville Slugger. I eyed where the bat was sleeping and revved the rake like I was going to hit a four-hundred-foot home run. Just before I swung I remembered another one of Bud Caldwell's Rules and Things for Having a Funner Life and Making a Better Liar Out of Yourself.

# RULES AND THINGS NUMBER 328

**When You Make Up Your Mind to Do Something,
Hurry Up and Do It, If You Wait You
Might Talk Yourself Out of What You
Wanted in the First Place.**

Shucks, I couldn't remember for sure if you killed a vampire by driving a stake in its heart or by shooting it with a silver bullet!

If I was wrong and didn't kill the bat right away I was going to be trapped in the shed with a vampire who was probably going to be real upset that someone had woke him up by whacking him with a rake.

I took my jackknife out of my pocket and pulled the blade open. That way if I didn't kill him with the rake and it came down to the two of us tussling on the floor maybe a silver blade in his heart would be just as good as a silver bullet. Unless that was what you had to do with werewolves.

I raised the rake over my head again, closed my eyes and swung it like I was Paul Bunyan chopping down a tree with one blow. I felt the rake jerk a little when it hit the bat and I opened my eyes just in time to see the vampire get cut right in half. I was kind of surprised it didn't scream or cry or say, "Curses, you got me!" Instead the only sound I heard was a kind of rattling like a couple of pieces of paper rubbing together or like dry leaves blowing around in the wind.

The next sound I heard was even worse than if the vampire had said, "Aha, you doggone kid, that hurt, but now I get my revenge!"

It sounded like I'd turned on a buzz saw in the shed. All of a sudden it felt like someone had stuck a red-hot nail right into my left cheek. My hand reached up to grab my cheek and I felt something creepy and prickly there. I brought my hand back down and it was holding the biggest, maddest hornet I'd ever seen. I squeezed my hand shut to crush it but it got in another sting on my palm.

What I'd thought was a vampire bat hanging on the ceiling was really a hornets' nest and now there were about six thousand hornets flying around in the tiny shed and each and every one of them was looking for me!

Another fire-nail went into my knee and a second one went into my sock. Maybe this was why the other kid that they'd found in here had been as big as a whale, he was swole up from all the hornet stings!

I dropped my shoulder down and charged at the door with all my might. The door banged against the lock but didn't budge a inch. All that happened was the rag I'd covered the fish heads with came off and I got bounced back and landed square on the floor. I jumped up again. This time when I charged at the door

I put my hand out like Paul Robeson running down the football field. This wasn't a real good idea, I forgot all about the fish-head door guards. My fingers went right into the mouth of the biggest one and his little needle teeth cut me like a razor. I pulled my hand back and screamed.

Another hornet buzzed into my ear and it felt like someone had poured hot wax right down into my brain.

The only thing I could think to do was jump on the woodpile and bust the glass out of the window. I grabbed the handles of the window and gave them one more jerk. I guess being scared gives you a lot of strength because this time the window flew open with a loud bang. Three hornets found me at the same time and all four of us fell out of the window.

As soon as we hit the ground I rolled as far away from the shed as I could go. I smacked and whacked the hornets that had taken a ride on me and just laid there until I could catch my breath.

After while the stings and the fish-guard bite quit hurting so much. I started getting madder and madder. I was mad at the Amoses, but most of all I was mad at me for believing there really was a vampire in the shed and for getting trapped like this where there wasn't anybody who cared what happened to me.

I simmered down and started thinking about getting even. I wondered how hard I'd have to pull the trigger on that double-barrel shotgun for it to go off. I sneaked up the back porch steps to get inside the house. Maybe the vampire bat didn't say it, but the only thought on my mind was, "Aha, you doggone Amoses, that hurt, but now I get my revenge!"

# CHAPTER 4

*THEY HADN'T LOCKED* the kitchen window. It slid open with just a couple of squeaks, then I was inside the Amos house crouched down like a cat burglar. Quick as a rabbit I looked under the table to see if they'd moved my suitcase. It was still there.

I got a whole lot calmer when I picked it up and it was the right weight, I didn't think they'd taken anything out of it. I couldn't be sure until I looked inside but I could do that later.

I took in a deep breath and looked over at the icebox to

see if the shotgun was still there. I let all the air out in a big puff when I saw it. Shucks, you'd think that with the Amoses being so doggone mean they'd worry about leaving a big old gun like that out in the open. What if one of their visitors got real mad at them about something?

I unlocked the back door and set my suitcase on the first step of the porch, so I could make a quick getaway after I was through paying these Amoses back.

I opened the screen door real quiet and went back into the house. Fair is fair. The Amoses deserved what they were going to get.

I can't all the way blame Todd for giving me trouble, though. If I had a regular home with a mother and father I wouldn't be too happy about other kids living in my house either.

Being unhappy about it is one thing, but torturing the kids who are there even though they don't want to be is another. It was my job to make sure other kids who didn't know where their mothers and fathers were didn't have to put up with Todd.

My heart started jumping around in my stomach as soon as I reached out for the shotgun.

It was a lot longer and heavier than I thought it would be.

I lifted it and felt how solid the smooth brown wood was against my shoulder. With it up close to my face like this I could smell the gray metal of the barrel and the gun oil Mr. Amos used on it.

I aimed the gun at the stove and pretended I was shooting at a elephant or a dragon or a tiger, or best of all, Todd!

I imagined how it would feel to creep up to his bed while he was sleeping and put the shotgun barrel right in his nose.

After that I'd have to do some quick moving to get the grown-up Amoses. Unless they were real sound sleepers the shotgun going off in Todd's room would give them a clue that something was going on.

I lowered the gun. These things were just too dangerous to play with or to take chances with, that's why the first part of my revenge plan was to get this gun out of the way.

If something went wrong and the Amoses woke up I didn't want them rushing down to the kitchen to get the gun. I knew they'd shoot me in a flash and tell the Home it was a accident.

I took the gun outside and put it on the back porch in a corner where they wouldn't be able to see it until daytime. I felt a lot better when it was out of my hands.

When I was back in the kitchen I started opening cupboards looking for the drinking glasses. The first one I opened had the jelly jar they'd given me to drink out of at suppertime.

I walked over to the sink and turned on one of the spigots. These Amoses had hot water running right into the house! I let it run for a second to warm up and put a dishrag in the bottom of the sink so the splashing wasn't too loud.

When the water was good and hot I stuck the jelly jar underneath until it was filled to the brim.

I started down the hall. Todd's door came open easy as anything.

I tiptoed over to his bed. He was deep asleep and his hands were crossed on his chest like he was ready for the graveyard.

I dipped my middle finger in the water. It felt like the perfect temperature.

I held my breath and picked up one of Todd's chubby hands.

One of the older boys at the Home told me if you dipped someone's hand in a warm glass of water whilst they're asleep they don't have any choice but to pee the bed. It's something about chemistry and biology making some valve in your guts open up and . . . woop, zoop, sloop . . . you got a wet bed.

I started to dip Todd's fingers in the water. But I couldn't dip more than two fingers at a time. Todd's bed stayed as dry as the desert.

I tried holding Todd's hand flat and pouring water over it but he still didn't wet the bed.

Finally I decided to just pour the water on his pajama pants.

I pulled the blanket and sheet down and emptied the jar.

His face twitched a couple of times and for a minute it

looked like his eyes were going to come open but they stayed shut. He smiled and the warm water from the jelly jar opened that little valve up and . . . woop, zoop, sloop . . . he soaked his sheets!

I tiptoed out of the room and down the hall and out the door.

My favorite saying in the whole world is "He who laughs last laughs best," so I put my hand over my mouth and whispered, "Ha-ha-ha."

I picked up my suitcase and walked to the street.

Man! I was on the lam, I was just like Public Enemy Number One. If J. Edgar Hoover and the FBI saw me now I'd be in some real serious hot water!

# CHAPTER 5

*BEING ON THE LAM* was a whole lot of fun . . . for about five minutes. Every time my heart beat I could feel the blood pushing hot and hard on the inside of my sting spots and the bite on my hand. But I couldn't let that slow me down, I had to get out of this neighborhood as quick as I could.

I knew a nervous-looking, stung-up kid with blood dripping from a fish-head bite and carrying a old raggedy suitcase didn't look like he belonged around here.

The only hope I had was the north side library. If I got

there maybe Miss Hill would be able to help me, maybe she'd understand and would be able to tell me what to do. And for now I could sneak into the library's basement to sleep.

It was a lot later than I'd ever been up before and I was kind of scared of the cops catching me. I had to be real careful, even if it was the middle of the night, even if I was crouching down, sneaking along the street like Pretty Boy Floyd.

At the library I walked past a row of giant Christmas trees that were planted on the side of the building. There was a door on the side with a light burning above it so I kept walking in the shadows made by the big trees. When I got to the back windows, I almost busted out crying. Somebody had gone and put big metal bars on the windows.

Even though I knew it was useless I tried tugging at the bars but they were the real McCoy, solid steel.

I headed back to the Christmas trees. They were low enough to the ground that no one could see me unless they were really looking, so I started opening my suitcase. Most folks don't have sense enough to carry a blanket around with them, but you never know when you might be sleeping under a Christmas tree at the library so I always keep mine handy.

I untied the strange knots that the Amoses had put in my twine and opened the suitcase. I could tell right away that someone had been fumbling through my things. First off, whenever I put the blanket in, I always fold it so that it stops all the other things from banging up against each other, but those doggone Amoses had just stuffed it in without paying no mind to what it was mashing up against.

I lifted the blanket out and saw that everything else was still there. You might be able to say that the Amoses were some mean old nosy folks, but you couldn't call them thieves.

I picked up the old tobacco bag that I keep my rocks in. I could tell by the way the drawstring was pulled that the Amoses had been poking through this too. I jiggled it up and down in my hand a couple of times and it felt like none of the rocks was missing but I opened it to count them anyway. None of them was gone.

Next I pulled Momma's picture out of the envelope I kept it in and held it so the light from the library's side door would shine down on it.

It looked like the Amoses hadn't hurt it. This was the only picture of Momma in the world. Running acrost the top of it was a sign that was writ on a long skinny flag, it said, BOYS AND GIRLS—FOLLOW THE GENTLE LIGHT TO THE MISS B. GOTTEN MOON PARK. Underneath the sign, between two big wagon wheels, was Momma.

She was about as old as I am now and was looking down and frowning. I can't understand why she was so unhappy, this park looked like the kind of place where you could have a lot of fun.

In the picture Momma was sitting on a real live little midget horse. It looked tired and dragged out like those big workhorses do, but it had a teeny-tiny body with a big sag where most horses have a straight back.

Momma was sitting right in the middle of the horse's back, riding him sidesaddle, except there wasn't any saddle so I guess you have to say she was riding him side-sag. She had two six-shooter pistols in her hands and the way her face looked you could tell she wished she could've emptied them on somebody. And I know who that somebody was. Momma told me it was her father, my granddad.

He'd gone and ruined everybody's fun that day by getting in a big fight with my mother about the gigantic white twenty-five-gallon Texas cowboy hat that she was wearing.

Momma used to tell me, "That hardheaded man insisted, insisted mind you, that I wear that horrible hat."

The hat was almost as big as Momma and you could see it was fake because as tall as it was no real cowboy could've wore it without getting it knocked off his head every time he rode under a tree or some telegraph wires.

Momma told me that some man used to drag the midget horse all through her neighborhood with a camera and if your momma or daddy signed a piece of paper he'd take some pictures of you, then come back in a couple of weeks so you could buy them. Momma wasn't looking like she had rocks in her jaw because the hat was so fake that a real cowboy would've laughed you out of town for wearing it, she was mad because the hat was so dirty.

When she used to tell me about it her eyes would get big and burny, like the whole thing happened the day before yesterday instead of all those years ago. She'd start moving around our apartment real quick, picking things up and putting them back in the exact same spot.

"Filth!" she'd say about the hat. "Absolute filth! Why, the thing was positively alive with germs! Who knows what type of people had worn it?"

I'd say, "I don't know, Momma."

She'd say, "Who knows how many years it had been worn by who knows how many sweaty little heads?"

I'd say, "I don't know, Momma."

She'd say, "The entire band on the inside was black and I'm sure it was crawling with ringworm, lice and tetters!"

I'd say, "Yes, Momma."

She'd say, "And that horrid little photographer didn't care, do you imagine it ever occurred to him to wash it?"

I'd say, "No, Momma."

She'd say, "Of course not, we meant less to him than that horse he mistreated so."

I'd say, "Yes, Momma."

She'd say, "But your grandfather insisted. To this day I cannot understand why, but he insisted, insisted . . ."

I'd say, "Yes, Momma."

We had that conversation a lot of times.

Me and Momma having the same conversations lots of times is one of the main things I can remember about her now. Maybe that's because when she'd tell me these things she used to squeeze my arms and look right hard in my face to make sure I was listening, but maybe I remember them because those arm-squeezing, face-looking times were the only times that things slowed down a little bit when Momma was around.

Everything moved very, very fast when Momma was near, she was like a tornado, never resting, always looking around us, never standing still. The only time stuff didn't blow around when she was near was when she'd squeeze my arms and tell me things over and over and over and over.

She had four favorite things to tell me, one of them was about the picture and another one was about my name.

She'd say, "Bud is your name and don't you ever let anyone call you anything outside of that either."

She'd tell me, "Especially don't you ever let anyone call you Buddy, I may have some problems but being stupid isn't one of them, I would've added that *dy* onto the end of your name if I intended for it to be there. I knew what I was doing, Buddy is a dog's name or a name that someone's going to use on you if they're being false-friendly. Your name is Bud, period."

I'd say, "OK, Momma."

And she'd say, every single time, "And do you know what a bud is?"

I always answered, "Yes, Momma," but it was like she didn't hear me, she'd tell me anyway.

"A bud is a flower-to-be. A flower-in-waiting. Waiting for just the right warmth and care to open up. It's a little fist of love waiting to unfold and be seen by the world. And that's you."

I'd say, "Yes, Momma."

I know she didn't mean anything by naming me after a flower, but it's sure not something I tell anybody about.

Another thing she'd tell me was, "Don't you worry, Bud, as soon as you get to be a young man I have a lot of things I'll explain to you." That didn't make me calm at all, that was Bud Caldwell's Rules and Things to Have a Funner Life and Make a Better Liar Out of Yourself Number 83.

### RULES AND THINGS NUMBER 83

**If a Adult Tells You Not to Worry, and
You Weren't Worried Before, You Better Hurry
Up and Start 'Cause You're Already Running Late.**

She'd tell me, "These things I'm going to explain to you later will be a great help for you." Then Momma'd look hard in my face, grab a holt of my arms real tight and say, "And Bud, I want you always to remember, no matter how bad things look to you, no matter how dark the night, when one door closes, don't worry, because another door opens."

I'd say, "What, it opens all by itself?"

She'd say, "Yes, it seems so."

That was it: "Another door opens." That was the thing that was supposed to have helped me. I should've known then that I was in for a lot of trouble.

It's funny how now that I'm ten years old and just about a man I can see how Momma was so wrong. She was wrong because she probably should've told me the things she thought I was too young to hear, because now that she's gone I'll never know what they were. Even if I was too young back then I could've rememorized them and used them when I did need help, like right now.

She was also wrong when she thought I'd understand that nonsense about doors closing and opening all by themselves. Back then it really scared me because I couldn't see what one door closing had to do with another one opening unless there was a ghost involved. All her talk made me start jamming a chair up against my closet door at night.

But now that I'm almost grown I see Momma wasn't talking about doors opening to let ghosts into your bedroom, she meant doors like the door at the Home closing leading to the door at the Amoses' opening and the door in the shed opening leading to me sleeping under a tree getting ready to open the next door.

I checked out the other things in my suitcase and they seemed OK. I felt a lot better.

Right now I was too tired to think anymore so I closed my suitcase, put the proper knots back in the twine, crawled under the Christmas tree and wrapped myself in the blanket.

I'd have to wake up real early if I wanted to get to the mission in time for breakfast, if you were one minute late they wouldn't let you in for food.

# CHAPTER 6

*UH-OH.* My eyes opened and I could see the sun behind the branch of a Christmas tree.

I jumped up, folded my blanket inside my suitcase, hid it and started running the six or seven blocks down to the mission.

I turned the corner and said, "Whew!" There were still people lined up waiting. I started walking along the line. The end was a lot farther away than I thought. The line turned all the way around two corners, then crossed over one street before I saw the last person. Shucks. I walked up to get behind him.

He said, "Line's closed. These here folks are the last ones." He pointed at a man standing next to a woman who was carrying a baby.

I said, "But sir . . ."

He said, "But nothing. Line's closed. These here folks are the last ones."

It was time to start lying. If I didn't get any food now I'd have to steal something out of someone's garbage or I wouldn't be able to eat until the mission opened for supper.

I said, "Sir, I—"

The man raised his hand and said, "Look, kid, everybody's got a story and everybody knows the rules. The line closes at seven o'clock. How's it fair to these people who been here since five o'clock that you can sleep until"—he looked at his wristwatch—"until seven-fifteen, then come busting down here expecting to eat? You think you got some kind of special privilege just 'cause you're skinny and raggedy? Look in the line, there's lots of folks look just like you, you ain't the worst.

"Supper starts at six P.M., but you see how things is, if you plan on getting fed you better be in line by four. Now get out of here before I get rough with you."

Shucks, being hungry for a whole day is about as bad as it can get. I said, "But . . ."

He reached in his pocket and pulled something out

that looked like a heavy black strap and slapped it across his hand. Uh-oh, here we go again.

He said, "That's it, no more talk, you opened your mouth one time too many. You rotten kids today don't listen to no one, but I'ma show you something that'll improve your hearing." He slapped the strap on his hand and started walking toward me.

I was wrong when I said being hungry for a day is about as bad as it can get, being hungry plus having a big knot on your head from a black leather strap would be even worse.

I backed away but only got two steps before I felt a giant warm hand wrap around my neck from behind. I looked up to see whose doggone hand was so doggone big and why they'd put it around my neck.

A very tall, square-shaped man in old blue overalls looked down at me and said, "Clarence, what took you so long?"

I got ready to say, "My name's not Clarence and please don't choke me, sir, I'll leave," but as soon as I opened my mouth he gave my head a shake and said, "I told you to hurry back, now where you been?" He gave me a shove and said, "Get back in line with your momma."

I looked up and down the line to see who was supposed to be my momma when a woman pointed her finger at her feet and said, "Clarence, you get over here right now." There were two little kids hanging on to her skirt.

I walked over to where she was and she gave me a good hard smack on the head. Shucks, for someone who was just pretending to be my momma she sure did slap me a good one.

I said, "Ow!"

The big square man who'd grabbed my neck looked at the man with the strap and said, "Boy had to go use the crapper, told him not to waste time, but like you said, these kids today don't listen to nobody."

The strap man looked at the size of the man who called me Clarence and walked back to the end of the line.

When the overall man got back in line I said, "Thank you, sir, I really tried to get—" But *he* popped me in the back of the head, hard, and said, "Next time don't be gone so long."

The two little kids busted out laughing and said, "Nyah-nyah-nyah-nyah-nyah, Clarence got a lickin', Clarence got a lickin'."

I told them, "Shut up, and don't call me—" Then *both* my pretend poppa and my pretend momma smacked my head.

She looked at the people direct behind us and said, "Mercy, when they get to be this age . . ."

The people weren't too happy about me taking cuts in the line, but when they looked at how big my pretend daddy was and they saw how hard him and my pretend momma were going upside my head they decided they wouldn't say anything.

I was grateful to these people, but I wished they'd quit popping me in the head, and it seems like with all the names in the world they could've come up with a better one for me than Clarence.

I stood in line with my pretend family for a long, long time. Everybody was very quiet about standing in line, even my pretend brother and sister and all the other kids. When we finally got around the last corner and could see the door and folks going in it seemed like a bubble busted and people started laughing and talking. The main thing people were talking about was the great big sign that was hanging over the building.

It showed a gigantic picture of a family of four rich white people sitting in a car driving somewhere. You could tell it was a family 'cause they all looked exactly alike. The only difference amongst them was that the daddy had a big head and a hat and the momma had the same head with a woman's hat and the girl had two big yellow pigtails coming out from above her ears. They all had big shiny teeth and big shiny eyes and big shiny cheeks and big shiny smiles. Shucks, you'd need to squint your eyes if that shiny family drove anywhere near you.

You could tell they were rich 'cause the car looked like it had room for eight or nine more people in it and 'cause they had movie star clothes on. The woman was wearing a coat with a hunk of fur around the neck and the man was wearing a suit and a tie and the kids looked like they were wearing ten-dollar-apiece jackets.

Writ about their car in fancy letters it said, THERE'S NO PLACE LIKE AMERICA TODAY!

My pretend daddy read it and said, "Uh-uh-uh, well, you got to give them credit, you wouldn't expect that they'd have the nerve to come down here and tell the truth."

When we finally got into the building it was worth the wait. The first thing you noticed when you got inside was how big the place was, and how many people were in it and how quiet it was. The only sound you could hear was when someone scraped a spoon across the bottom of their bowl or pulled a chair in or put one back or when the people in front of you dragged their feet on the floor moving up to where they were spooning out the food.

After we'd picked up our spoons and bowls a lady dug a big mess of oatmeal out of a giant pot and swopped it down into our bowls. She smiled and said, "I hope you enjoy."

Me and my pretend family all said, "Thank you, ma'am." Then a man put two pieces of bread and a apple and a big glass of milk on your tray and said, "Please read the signs to your children. Thank you."

We all said, "Thank you, sir." Then we walked past some signs someone'd stuck up on the wall.

One said, PLEASE DO NOT SMOKE, another said, PLEASE EAT AS QUICKLY AND QUIETLY AS POSSIBLE, another one said, PLEASE BE CONSIDERATE AND PATIENT—CLEAN UP

AFTER YOURSELF—YOUR NEIGHBORS WILL BE EATING AFTER YOU, and the last one said, WE ARE TERRIBLY SORRY BUT WE HAVE NO WORK AVAILABLE.

My pretend daddy read the signs to my pretend brother and sister and we all sat at a long table with strangers on both sides of us.

The oatmeal was delicious! I poured some of my milk into it so it wouldn't be so lumpy and mixed it all together.

My pretend mother opened her pocketbook and took out a little brown envelope. She reached inside of it and sprinkled something on my pretend brother's and sister's oatmeal, then said to them, "I know that's not as much as you normally get, but I wanted to ask you if you minded sharing some with Clarence."

They pouted and gave me a couple of dirty looks. My pretend mother said, "Good," and emptied the rest of the envelope over my oatmeal. Brown sugar!

Shucks, I didn't even mind them calling me Clarence anymore. I said "Thank you, Momma, ma'am."

She and my pretend daddy laughed and he said, "It took you long enough to catch on, Clarence." He acted like he was going to smack me again but he didn't.

After we'd finished all our food we put our bowls up and I thanked my pretend family again, I asked them, "Are you going to be coming back for supper?"

My pretend momma said, "No, dear, we only come here mornings. But you make sure you get here plenty early, you hear?"

I said, "Yes, Momma, I mean, ma'am."

I watched them walking away. My pretend brother looked back at me and stuck out his tongue, then reached up and took my pretend mother's hand. I couldn't really blame him, I don't think I'd be real happy about sharing my brown sugar and my folks with any strange kids either.

# CHAPTER 7

*I PUSHED* the heavy door open and walked into the library. The air in the library isn't like the air anywhere else, first it's always cooler than the air outside, it feels like you're walking into a cellar on a hot July day, even if you have to walk up a bunch of stairs to get into it.

The next thing about the air in the library is that no other place smells anything like it. If you close your eyes and try to pick out what it is that you're sniffing you're only going to get confused, because all the smells have blended together and turned themselves into a different one.

As soon as I got into the library I closed my eyes and took a deep breath. I got a whiff of the leather on all the old books, a smell that got real strong if you picked one of them up and stuck your nose real close to it when you turned the pages. Then there was the smell of the cloth that covered the brand-new books, the books that made a splitting sound when you opened them. Then I could sniff the paper, that soft, powdery, drowsy smell that comes off the pages in little puffs when you're reading something or looking at some pictures, a kind of hypnotizing smell.

I think it's that smell that makes so many folks fall asleep in the library. You'll see someone turn a page and you can imagine a puff of page powder coming up really slow and easy until it starts piling on the person's eyelashes, weighing their eyes down so much that they stay down a little longer after each blink and finally making them so heavy that they just don't come back up at all. Then their mouths come open and their heads start bouncing up and down like they're bobbing in a big tub of water for apples and before you know it, . . . woop, zoop, sloop . . . they're out cold and their face thunks down smack-dab on the book.

That's the part that gets the librarians the maddest, they get real upset if folks start drooling in the books and, page powder or not, they don't want to hear no excuses, you gotta get out. Drooling in the books is even worse than laughing out loud in the library, and even though it might seem kind of mean, you can't really blame the librarians for tossing drooly folks out 'cause there's nothing worse than opening a book and having the pages all stuck together from somebody's dried-up slobber.

I opened my eyes to start looking for Miss Hill. She wasn't at the lending desk so I left my suitcase with the white lady there. I knew it would be safe.

I walked between the stacks to see if Miss Hill was putting books up. Three doggone times I walked through the library, upstairs and down, and couldn't find her.

I went back up to the librarian at the lending desk. I waited until she looked up at me. She smiled and said, "Yes? Would you like to retrieve your suitcase?" She reached under the desk.

I said, "Not yet, ma'am, could I ask you a question?"

She said, "Of course, young man, how may I help you?"

"I'm looking for Miss Hill."

The librarian looked surprised. "Miss Hill? My goodness, hadn't you heard?"

Uh-oh! That's Number 16 of Bud Caldwell's Rules and Things for Having a Funner Life and Making a Better Liar Out of Yourself, that's one of the worst ones.

## RULES AND THINGS NUMBER 16

**If a Grown-up Ever Starts a Sentence by Saying
"Haven't You Heard," Get Ready, 'Cause
What's About to Come Out of Their Mouth Is Gonna
Drop You Headfirst into a Boiling Tragedy.**

It seems like the answer to "Haven't you heard" always has something to do with someone kicking the bucket. And not kicking the bucket in a calm, peaceful way like a heart attack at home in bed either, it usually is some kind of dying that will make your eyes buck out of your head when you hear about it, it's usually the kind of thing that will run you out of a room with your hands over your ears and your mouth wide open.

Something like hearing that your grandmother got her whole body pulled through the wringer on a washing machine, or something like hearing about a horse slipping on the ice and landing on some kid you went to school with.

I answered, "No, ma'am," and got my stomach ready to hear about Miss Hill biting the dust in some way that was going to give me nightmares.

The librarian said, "There's no need for you to look so stricken. It's not bad news, young man."

She laughed a quiet, librarian-type laugh and said, "Really, it's not bad news. Unless you had matrimonial plans concerning Miss Hill."

I pretended I knew what she was talking about, most times if you listen to how grown folks ask a question they let you know what it is they want to hear.

I said, "No, ma'am, I didn't plan that at all."

She laughed again and said, "Good, because I don't think her new husband would appreciate the competition. Charlemae . . . Miss Hill is currently living in Chicago, Illinois."

I said, "Husband? You mean she got married, ma'am?"

The librarian said, "Oh, yes, and I must tell you, she was radiating happiness."

I said, "And she moved all the way to Chicago?"

"That's right, but Chicago isn't that far. Here, I'll show you."

She reached under her desk and pulled out a thick leather book called *Atlas of the United States of America.*

She thumbed through a couple of pages and said, "Here we are." She turned the book to me, it was a big map of Michigan and a couple of the states that were next to it.

"We're here." She pointed to the spot that said Flint. "And Chicago is here in Illinois."

They looked pretty close, but I know how tricky maps can be, shucks, they can put the whole world on one page on a map, so I said, "How long would it take someone to walk that far?"

She said, "Oh, dear, quite a while, I'm afraid. Let's check the distance."

She reached under the desk and pulled out another thick book called *Standard Highway Mileage Guide* and turned to a page that had a million numbers and city names on it. She showed me how to find Chicago on the line that was running across the page and Flint on the line that was running down the page and then to look at the number that was writ where the two of them joined up. It said 270.

She pulled a pencil out and said, "OK, this is how one figures the amount of time required to walk to Chicago. Now—" She pulled a third book out.

Shucks, this is one of the bad things about talking to librarians, I asked one question and already she had us digging through three different books.

She thumbed through the book until she said, "Aha, it says here that the average male human gait is five miles an hour. OK, assuming that you could cover five miles an hour, all we have to do is divide two hundred seventy by five."

She did it and said, "Fifty-four hours! Much too long to be practical. No, I'm afraid you'll simply have to wait until Mrs. Rollins comes back to Flint for a visit."

Shucks. Chicago might as well be a million miles away from Flint and Miss Hill might as well be a squashed, crunched-up mess in a washing machine when it came down to helping me now.

I thanked the librarian for the bad news and went to

sit at one of the big heavy tables so I could think what to do next.

Going back to the Home was out, it used to be that we'd get a new kid every once in a while, but lately it seems like there's a couple of new kids every day, mostly babies, and they're most always sick. It's not like it was when I first got there, shucks, half the folks that run it don't even tell you their name and don't remember yours unless you're in trouble all the time or getting ready to move out.

After while I got my suitcase and walked into the regular air and stinking smells of Flint.

That library door closing after I walked out was the exact kind of door Momma had told me about. I knew that since it had closed the next one was about to open.

I went back under my tree and before I knew it I was asleep.

# CHAPTER 8

SOMETHING STEPPED on a little stick. As soon as the twig cracked my eyes snapped open and I was wide awake. I held my breath and kept as still as I could. Whatever it was that was sneaking up on me knew I'd woked up 'cause it stopped moving and kept as still as it could too. Even though my head was still under my blanket, I could feel two eyes staring at me real hard, and I knew these weren't critter eyes, these eyes made the hair on the back of my neck raise up the way only human bean eyes can do.

Without wiggling or jiggling around too much under my blanket I got my fingers wrapped around my jackknife. Right when I was ready to push the covers off of me and start running or stabbing, whoever it was that had been watching jumped right on top of me. I was as trapped as a roach under a dishrag!

I tried to guess the exact spot that the person's heart was at, then pulled my knife back. A voice said, "If you ain't a kid called Bud from the Home I'm really sorry about jumping on you like this!"

It was Bugs!

When I tried to talk it felt like I had to suck all the air out of Flint, I finally got breathing right and said, "Doggone it, Bugs, it *is* me! You nearly scared me to death!"

He got off of me and I threw the blanket over to the side. "You don't know how lucky you are, I was just about fixing to stab you in the heart!"

Bugs looked like he knew he'd just had a real close call. He said, "I'm sorry, Bud, I didn't mean to scare you, but everybody knows how you like to sleep with that knife open so I figured I'd best grab holt of you so's you wouldn't wake up slicing nobody."

Shucks, even though it was Bugs who'd come real close to getting his heart poked, I was the one who was still having trouble catching my breath.

I asked, "How come you aren't back at the Home?" But before he had a chance to answer I knew. "You're on the lam."

Bugs said, "Yup, I'm going back to riding the rails. When I heard about you beating that kid up so bad that you had to take off I figured it was time for me to get going too. I thought you might be hanging around the library so I come down to see if you wanted to go with me."

"Where you heading?"

"There's always fruits to be picked out west, I heard we can make enough money to get by out there. There's supposed to be a train leaving sometime tomorrow. Did you really beat that kid up in the foster home?"

I said, "Uh-huh, we kind of had a fight. How long's it take to get out west?"

Bugs said, "Depends on how many trains you got to hop. Was he really two years older than you?"

"Uh-huh, he was twelve. Is it fun to hop a train?"

"Some of the time it is, some of the time it's scary. We heard he was kind of big too, was he?"

I said, "He was pretty big. I can't see how we can hop on a train, they look like they're moving pretty doggone fast."

Bugs said, "Most times you don't hop them when they're going fast, most times you try to climb on one when it's sitting in the train yard. Did the guy cry after you whupped him?"

"Well, kind of, he looked real scared, then told his momma to keep me away from him. They even said I was a hoodlum. Will we be sleeping on the train and everything?"

"Sure we will. Some of the time the train don't stop for two or three days. Man, I always try to tell people that just because someone's skinny it don't mean they can't fight, you're a hero now, Bud!"

"Naw, I didn't really do nothing much. Well, how 'bout the toilet? How we going to use the toilet if the train doesn't stop?"

Bugs said, "You just kind of lean out of the door and go."

"When the train is still moving?"

"Yeah. You get a real nice breeze."

"Oh, man! That sounds great! Count me in, I can't wait!"

Bugs spit a big glob of slob in his hand and said, "I knew I could depend on you, Bud."

I spit a big glob in my hand and said, "We're brothers forever, Bugs!"

We slapped our hands together as hard as we could and got our slobs mixed up real good, then waved them in the air so they'd dry. Now it was official, I finally had a brother!

Bugs said, "We'll go down to the mission. There's bound to be someone there that knows about where we can hop this train, then we'll be on the lam together!"


WE FOUND OUT that we'd have to go to a city called Hooperville just outside of Flint. The only trouble was nobody knew exactly where Hooperville was. It was dark before we found out the right direction. I'd never heard of a city that was so doggone hard to find.

We walked on a trail through some woods that run right up against Thread Crick. We could tell we were getting close to Hooperville 'cause we heard somebody playing a mouth organ and the smell of food cooking was getting stronger. We kept walking in the direction that the sky was glowing with a orangeish light.

When we could hear the music real clear, and folks talking to each other and the sound of sticks cracking in a fire, we started cutting through the trees. That way we could peek into Hooperville first.

We looked out from behind a big tree and saw that a big wind or even two or three big wolves huffing and puffing real hard could blow Hooperville into the next county. It was a bunch of huts and shacks throwed together out of pieces of boxes and wood and cloth. The Amoses' shed would've looked like a real fancy house here.

Right near our tree was the big fire that had been lighting up the sky. It looked like a hundred people were sitting around it, watching things burn or waiting for the food cooking in three big pots set up in the fire.

There were two littler fires burning in Hooperville. One had a pot that was big enough to boil a whole person in it. A man was stirring things in the pot with a big stick and when he raised the stick up he'd pull some britches or a shirt out and pass it over to a white man who was hanging the clothes on a line to dry. There was a mountain of clothes on the ground next to him waiting on their turn.

The other fire in Hooperville was real small. It was off to the side, by itself. There were five white people sitting at this fire, two kids, a man, and a woman holding a little wrapped-up baby. The baby sounded like all those new sick babies at the Home, it was coughing like it was a half-dead little animal.

Bugs whispered, "Shoot, this ain't no city, this is just another cardboard jungle."

"A what?"

"A cardboard jungle, somewhere you can get off the train and clean up and get something to eat without the cops chasing you out of town."

I said, "Well, what're we going to do? We can't just go busting into this city and expect someone to feed us, can we?"

Bugs said, "One of us has got to talk to them, let's flip for it."

"OK."

Bugs rumbled around in his pocket and found a penny. He rubbed it up against his britches and said, "Heads I win, tails you lose."

"OK."

He flipped the penny up into the air and caught it, then slapped it down on the back of his left hand.

He peeked underneath his right hand to see and a big smile cracked his face. Shucks!

Bugs said, "Tails. You lose."

"Dang! So what should I say?"

"Ask them if this is Hooperville, see if they got any extra food."

I moved out from behind our tree and walked over toward the biggest fire, I waited until some folks noticed me, then said, "Excuse me, is this here Hooperville?"

The man who was playing the mouth organ stopped and everyone else around the fire looked up at me.

One of the white men said, "What is it you looking for?"

I said, "A city called Hooperville, sir."

They all laughed.

The mouth organ man said, "Naw, son, what you're looking for is Hooverville, with a *v*, like in President Herbert Hoover."

I said, "Oh, is this it, sir?"

The man said, "This is one of them."

I said, "One of them?"

He answered, "They're all over the country, this here is the Flint version."

"And all of them are called Hooverville?"

"That's right, Mr. Hoover worked so hard at making sure every city has got one that it seems like it would be criminal to call them anything else."

Someone said, "That's the truth!"

I said, "Well, how're we going to know if we're in the right one?"

The mouth organ man said, "Are you hungry?"

"Yes, sir."

"Are you tired?"

"Yes, sir."

"Are you scared about what's going to happen tomorrow?"

I didn't want anyone to think I was a baby so I said, "Not exactly scared, sir, maybe I am a little bit nervous."

The man smiled and said, "Well, son, anyplace where there're other folks in need of the same things that you are is the right place to be. This is *exactly* the Hooverville you're looking for."

I knew what the man was trying to say. This was the exact same kind of circle-talking and cross-talking that Momma used to do. Bugs hadn't had that kind of practice, he came from behind the tree and said, "I don't get it, you said there were Hoovervilles all over the place, what if we was looking for the Hooverville in Detroit or Chicago, how could this be the right one to be in?"

The man said, "You boys from Flint?"

I said, "Yes, sir."

The man waved his mouth organ like a magic wand and pointed it all over the little cardboard city.

"Boys," he said, "look around you."

The city was bigger than I thought it was. The raggedy little huts were in every direction you looked.

And there were more people sitting around than I first thought too, mostly it was men and big boys, but there were a couple of women every now and then and a kid or two. They were all the colors you could think of, black, white and brown, but the fire made everyone look like they were different shades of orange. There were dark orange folks sitting next to medium orange folks sitting next to light orange folks.

"All these people," the mouth organ man said, "are just like you, they're tired, hungry and a little bit nervous about tomorrow. This here is the right place for y'all to be 'cause we're all in the same boat. And you boys are nearer to home than you'll ever get."

Someone said, "Amen, brother."

The mouth organ man said, "It don't matter if you're looking for Chicago or Detroit or Orlando or Oklahoma City, I rode the rails to all of them. You might think or you might hear that things are better just down the line, but they're singing the same sad song all over this country. Believe me, son, being on the road is no good. If you two boys are from Flint, this is the right Hooverville for you."

Someone said, "Brother, why don't we feed these boys? That one looks like he ain't et in two or three months."

Shucks, he didn't have to point or nothing, everyone knew who he meant.

But I didn't care, the food that was bubbling up in those three big pots even sounded delicious.

The mouth organ man said, "You're welcome to join us, but we all pitch in here, so's unless either one of you is carrying one of them smoked West Virginny hams in them bags, it looks like you'll be pulling KP tonight."

I said, "Pulling what, sir?"

He said, "KP, Kitchen Police, you do the cleanup after everyone's had their fill. There're a couple of other young folks who'll show you what you have to do."

Me and Bugs both said, "Yes, sir!" This seemed like a real good trade.

A woman handed me and Bugs each a flat, square, empty tin can. "That, m'lords, is your china. Please be careful not to chip it."

My china had the words JUMBO A&P SARDINES stamped into the bottom of it.

She handed us two beat-up old spoons and said, "Don't be shy, you two just about missed supper, you'd best hurry up."

She took us over to one of the big pots and filled up our tin plates.

"You're lucky," she said, "it's muskrat stew and there's plenty left over tonight, eat as much as you can."

The stew was made out of dandelion greens and a couple of potatoes and some small wild carrots and some crawdads and a couple of little chunks of meat. It tasted great! We both even got seconds!

When we were done, the woman told us, "You boys leave your bags here, it's time to do the dishes now."

Uh-oh. "Ma'am, I like to keep my suitcase with me wherever I go."

"I promise you your suitcase will be safe here."

I remembered the Amoses had promised the same thing. I said, "You'll watch it yourself, ma'am? You'll make sure no one looks inside of it?"

She said, "Son, we don't have no thieving in here, we all look out for each other."

I said, "Thank you, ma'am," and put my suitcase down near the woman's feet.

Me, Bugs, a little white boy and a little girl loaded a whole mess of dirty tin cans and spoons and a couple of real plates and forks into a big wooden box and lugged them down to Thread Crick.

The little girl had been in Hooverville the longest so she got to tell the rest of us what to do. She said, "I don't suppose neither one of you new boys knows how to do dishes the right way, do you?"

Me and Bugs had done tons of dishes in the Home so I said, "Sure we do, we used to be real good at cleaning up."

Bugs said, "Dang, girl, you act like this is the first cardboard jungle I've been in, I know how you do dishes out here."

She said, "OK then, we'll split them up, you and you"—she pointed at Bugs and the other kid—"can do half, and me and this boy can do the others. What's your name?"

I said, "Bud, not Buddy."

She said, "I'm Deza Malone."

Deza handed Bugs and the other little boy some rags and some soap powder and they started splashing the dishes in the water.

Me and the girl walked a little farther up the crick and started unloading the rest of the dishes. "You dry, I'll wash," she said.

She handed me a rag and just as soon as she'd splashed one of the tin cans in the water and give it to me I'd dry it and stick it in the wooden box.

She said, "Where you say you was from?"

"Flint, right here."

"So, you and your friend come down here to get on that train tomorrow?"

"Where's it going?"

"Chicago," she said.

"Is that west from here?"

"Uh-huh."

"Then yup, that's where we're heading," I said. "Where you from?"

"Lancaster, Pennsylvania."

"You going to take the train too?"

She said, "Uh-uh. My daddy is. Folks say there's work out west so he's going to try again."

"So you're going to wait here for him?"

"Uh-huh."

She was real fast at washing the dishes but I noticed

she got kind of slow and was touching my hand a lot when it came to giving them to me.

She said, "Where's your momma and daddy?"

"My mother died four years ago."

"Sorry to hear that."

"It's OK, she didn't suffer or nothing."

"So where's your daddy?"

"I think he lives in Grand Rapids, I never met him."

"Sorry to hear that." Shucks, she held right on to my hand when she said that. I squirmed my hand a-loose and said, "That's OK too."

Deza said, "No it's not, and you should quit pretending that it is."

"Who said I'm pretending anything?"

"I know you are, my daddy says families are the most important thing there is. That's why me and my momma are going to wait together for him to come back or write for us to come to him."

I said, "My mother said the same thing, that families should be there for each other all the time. She always used to tell me that no matter where I went or what I did that she'd be there for me, even if she wasn't somewhere that I could see her. She told me . . ."

Shucks, there're some folks who'll have you running your mouth before you know what you're doing. I quit talking and acted like I was having a real hard time drying the tin can she'd just handed me.

"What'd she tell you, Bud?"

I looked at Deza Malone and figured I'd never see her again in my life so I kept shooting off my mouth. "She would tell me every night before I went to sleep that no matter what happened I could sleep knowing that there had never been a little boy, anywhere, anytime, who was loved more than she loved me. She told me that as long as I remembered that I'd be OK."

"And you knew it was the truth."

"Just as much as I know my name's Bud, not Buddy."

She said, "Don't you have no other kin here in Flint?"

"No."

"I guess I can't blame you for wanting to ride the rails. My momma says these poor kids on the road all alone are like dust in the wind. But I guess you're different, aren't you, Bud? I guess you sort of carry your family around inside of you, huh?"

"I guess I do. Inside my suitcase, too."

She said, "So you been staying in a orphanage since your momma died?"

"What makes you say that?"

"Well, you're kind of skinny, but I can tell by the way you talk and the way you act that you haven't been out on the road for very long. You still look young."

I said, "Shucks, I'm not all that young, I'm going to be eleven on November fourteenth, and I'm not skinny, I'm wiry. Some folks think I'm a hero."

"So, Mr. Hero, we're the same age. But you have been staying in a orphanage."

"I been staying in a home."

"My daddy says being on the road ain't fit for a dog, much less a kid, how come you don't just go back to your orphanage?" She started up touching my hand too much again.

Deza Malone seemed like she was all right so I came clean with her. "Don't tell no one, but I lit out from a foster home so I'm on the lam. And I wouldn't go back to the Home even if I could. It's getting so's there's too many kids in there."

"So? That's better than being cold and hungry all the time and dodging the railroad police."

"What do you mean?"

"You don't think they just let people jump on the trains, do you?"

"Well, I guess I hadn't thought about it."

"See, I knew you were too nice to have been out on the road, you're going to have a bad surprise tomorrow morning."

"That won't bother me too much."

She said, "Oh, yeah, I forgot, you're a hero to some folks." When Deza smiled a little dimple jumped up in her brown cheek.

I didn't answer, I just kept drying tin cans.

We got to the last four or five tin can plates and Deza said, "You ever kiss a girl at the orphanage?"

Uh-oh! "Are you kidding?"

"No. Why, you afraid of girls?"

"You must be kidding."

She said, "OK," and closed her eyes and mooshed her lips up and leaned close to me.

Dangee! If I didn't kiss her she'd think I was scared of girls, if I did kiss her she might blab or Bugs might see me and tell strangers about what happened. I looked down the crick to where Bugs and the other boy were still splashing in the water. It was dark enough that I didn't think they could see us too good.

I scooched my lips up and mashed my face on Deza Malone's. We stuck like that for a hot second, but it felt like a long time.

When I opened my eyes and pulled back Deza kept hers closed and smiled. She looked down and stuck her hand in mine again and this time I let her keep it there. She looked out at the crick and the woods on the other side and said, "Isn't this romantic?"

I looked out to see what she was talking about. The only thing I could see was the moon like a big egg yolk way up in the sky. You could hear the water and the sound of the mouth organ man playing a sad song back in Hooverville. I sneaked another peek at Deza's dimple.

She said, "You hear that? That's 'Shenandoah' he's playing. Isn't it pretty?"

"I guess so."

"Do you know the words?"

"Uh-uh."

"Listen.

> *It's been seven long years*
> *Since last I've seen her,*
> *Way hey, you rolling river,*
> *Been seven long years,*
> *Since last I've seen her,*
> *Way hey, I'm bound away,*
> *'Cross the wide Miss-oo-ray."*

I said, "Yup, that's a sad song." I didn't think it was pretty at all.

She squeezed my hand and said, "Isn't it? It's about an Indian man and woman who can't see each other for seven years. But in all that time they still stay in love, no matter what happens. It reminds me of my mother and father."

"Your dad's been gone for seven years before?"

She looked out over the crick like the big eggy moon had her hypnotized. I pulled my hand from hers and said, "Well, that's just about it for the dishes."

She smiled again. "Bud, I'll never forget this night."

I didn't tell her, but I probably wouldn't forget it either, I'd practiced on the back of my hand before, but this was the first time I'd ever busted slob with a real live girl.

We loaded all the dishes in the box and walked down to Bugs and the other kid. We put their dishes on top of ours and headed back.

76

Bugs said, "How come you're looking so strange, Bud? You look like you been chunked in the head with a rock."

Deza Malone laughed, and for a second I thought she was going to rat me out.

I said, "I don't know, I guess that song is making me kind of sad."

Bugs said, "Yeah, it is kind of sad."

Right before we got into the cardboard jungle we passed the white people with the coughing baby at their own little fire. I said to Deza, "How come they're off alone, they aren't allowed to sit around the big fire 'cause that baby's making so much noise?"

Deza said, "Uh-uh, they been invited, but my daddy said you got to feel sorry for them. All they're eating is dandelion greens soup, they're broke, their clothes are falling off of them, their baby's sick but when someone took them some food and blankets, the man said, 'Thank you very much, but we're white people. We ain't in need of a handout.' "

When we got back to the main fire of Hooverville we put the dishes in another box. Deza made us turn them all upside down so's if the rain got into them they wouldn't rust.

I went to the woman with my suitcase. It was in the same spot I'd left it and the knots in the twine were the kind I tie.

I said, "Thank you very much, ma'am."

She said, "I told you not to worry."

I went back to the big fire to sit with Bugs.

The mouth organ man said, "I suppose you boys are going out on that train tomorrow?"

I said, "The one for Chicago, sir?"

He said, "That's the one."

I said, "Yes, we are, sir."

He said, "Well, you'd best get as much sleep as you can. It's supposed to be pulling out at five-fifteen, but you never know with these freights."

We got in one of the shacks with some other boys. Bugs was snoring in two seconds, but I couldn't sleep, I opened my jackknife and put it under my blanket.

I was thinking. Deza's momma was right, someone who doesn't know who their family is, is like dust blowing around in a storm, they don't really belong any one place. I started wondering if going to California was the right thing to do. I might not know who my family was, but I knew they were out there somewhere, and it seemed to make a whole lot more sense to think that they were somewhere around Flint instead of out west.

I opened my suitcase to get my blanket. Even though I trusted the woman who'd guarded it for me I checked to make sure everything was OK.

I picked up the tobacco pouch that had my rocks in it and pulled the drawstring open. I shook the five smooth stones out and looked at them. They'd been in the drawer after the ambulance took Momma away and I'd had them ever since.

Someone had took a pen or something and had writ on all five of them, but it was writ in a code so I couldn't understand what they meant. One of them said "kentland ill. 5.10.11." Another said "loogootee in. 5.16.11," then there was "sturgis m. 8.30.12" and "gary in. 6.13.12," and the last one said, "flint m. 8.11.11."

I put them back in their pouch and pulled the string tight. Then I pulled out the envelope that had the picture of the saggy pony at the Miss B. Gotten Moon Park. It was fine.

Next I counted the flyers again, all five were there, I slid all of them back, except for the blue one. I held it up so it could catch some of the light from the big fire. I kept looking at the picture and wondering why this one bothered Momma so much. The more I thought about it the more I knew this man just had to be my father. Why else would Momma keep these?

I used a little trick to help me fall off to sleep. I pulled my blanket right up over my head and breathed in the smell real deep. After doing this three times the smells of the shack and Hooverville were gone and only the smell of the blanket was in my nose. And that smell always reminded me of Momma and how she used to read me to sleep every night.

I took two more breaths and pretended I was hearing Momma reading to me about the Billy Goats Gruff or the Fox and the Grapes or the Dog That Saw His Reflection in the Water or some other story she'd checked out of the library. I could hear Momma's voice getting farther and farther away as I imagined I was in the story until finally her voice and the story all mixed into one.

I'd learned that it was best to be asleep before Momma finished the story because if she got done and I was still awake she'd always tell me what the story was about. I never told Momma, but that always ruint the fun of the story. Shucks, here I was thinking I was just hearing something funny about a fox or a dog and Momma spoilt it by telling me they were really lessons about not being greedy or not wishing for things you couldn't have.

I took two more breaths and started thinking about the little hen that baked the bread. I heard, "Not I," said the pig. "Not I," said the goat. "Not I," said the big bad wolf," then . . . woop, zoop, sloop . . . I was asleep.

I started dreaming about the man with the giant fiddle. He was walking away and I kept calling him but he couldn't look back. Then the dream got a lot better, I turned away from where Herman E. Calloway was and there stood Deza Malone.

I told her, "I really like your dimple." She laughed and said, "See you in seven years."


A MAN SCREAMED, "Get up, they're trying to sneak it out early!" I jumped straight up and banged my head on the top of the shack. I ran outside. It was still dark and the fire was just a pile of glowing sticks. The man was screaming at the top of his lungs. "Get up! They've fired the engine and are fixing to take off!"

Bugs and the other boys came and stood next to me. Bugs said, "Is it a raid?"

Someone said, "No, they're trying to sneak out before we get up!"

People started running all over Hooverville. Bugs said, "Come on, Bud, get your stuff, we got to get on that train!"

I folded my blanket up and put it in my suitcase and tied the twine back. I put my jackknife in my pocket and Bugs and I ran outside. I hadn't got six giant steps away when a boy stuck his head out the door and yelled, "Hey, Slim, is this your paper?"

I looked back. My blue flyer! I forgot to put it back in the suitcase!

Bugs said, "Hurry, I'll wait."

"I'll catch you, go ahead."

I ran back and took my flyer from the boy. "Thanks a lot!" I ran back out into the crowd that was tearing through the woods. There were a million men and boys running in the same direction.

I didn't want to fold the flyer up so as I was running I slid it between the twine and the suitcase, I'd put it back inside once we got on the train.

No one was talking. All you could hear were the

sounds of a million feet smacking on the trail and the sound of a million people trying to catch their breath. Finally a hiss sound started getting louder and louder and I knew we weren't too far away.

We broke out of the woods and there in the dark sat the train. The locomotive was hissing and spitting coal-black smoke into the sky, every once in a while a big shower of sparks would glow up from inside the dark cloud, making it look like a gigantic black genie was trying to raise up out of the smokestack. The train went as far back as you could see, there must've been a thousand boxcars, but everyone had stopped and was just standing there watching. No one was trying to get on.

I pushed my way to the front to see if I could find Bugs and I saw why everyone had stopped. There were four cop cars and eight cops standing between the crowd and the train. The cops all had billy clubs and were spread out to protect the train.

The crowd kept getting bigger and bigger.

One of the cops yelled, "You men know you can't get on this train, just go on back to Shantytown and there won't be no trouble."

A white man said, "This is the only train going west for the next month, you know we got families to feed and have got to be on it. You go get back in your cars and you'll be right, there won't be no trouble."

The cop said, "I'm warning you, the Flint police are

on the way, this here is private property and they have orders to shoot anyone who tries to get on this train."

A man next to me said, "I'd rather be shot than sit around and watch my kids go hungry."

The cop said, "This is America, boys, you're sounding like a bunch of Commies, you know I can't let you on this train. I got kids to feed too, and I'd lose my job."

Someone yelled, "Well, welcome to the club, brother."

It seemed like we stood looking at the cops and them looking at us for a whole hour. Our side was getting bigger and bigger and the other cops started looking nervous. The one who was doing all the talking saw them fidgeting and said, "Hold steady, men."

One of the cops said, "Jake, there's four hundred men out there and more coming, I don't like these odds. Mr. Pinkerton ain't paying me enough to do this." He threw his cop hat and his billy club on the ground.

Everybody froze when the train whistle blew one long time and the engine started saying *shuh-shuh-shuh.* The big steel wheels creaked a couple of times, then started moving.

Four of the other cops threw their hats and billy clubs down too. The boss cop said, "You lily-livered rats," and it was like someone said, "On your mark, get set, go!"

The engine was saying *SHUHSHUHSHUHSHUH-SHUH* . . . and a million boys and men broke for the train.

I got pushed from behind and fell on top of my suitcase. Someone reached down and pulled me up. I squeezed my bag to my stomach and ran. The train was going faster and faster. People were jumping on and reaching back to help others. I finally got to the tracks and was running as hard as I could. I looked up into the boxcar and saw Bugs.

He screamed, "Bud, throw your bag, throw me your bag!"

I used both hands to throw my suitcase at the train. Bugs caught it and when he set it behind him the blue flyer blew out of the twine and fluttered outside the door. But it was like a miracle, the flyer flipped over three times and landed right in my hand. I slowed down and put it in my pocket.

Bugs reached one arm out and screamed, "Bud, don't stop! Run!"

I started running again but it felt like my legs were gone. The car with Bugs in it was getting farther and farther away. Finally I stopped.

Bugs was leaning out of the door and stopped reaching back for me. He waved and disappeared into the boxcar. A second later my suitcase came flying out of the door.

I walked over to where it landed and picked it up. Man, this is one tough suitcase, you couldn't even tell what it had been through, it still looked exactly the same.

I sat on the side of the tracks and tried to catch my breath.

The train and my new pretend brother got farther and farther away, chugging to Chicago. Man, I'd found some family and he was gone before we could really get to know each other.

There were six or seven other people who didn't make the train, so we all walked back toward Hooverville. They must've lit the big fire again, the sky in that direction was glowing orange.

The cop that first threw down his billy club walked over to us and said, "He wasn't lying about the Flint police coming, but they're coming to bust up the shantytown, you all should get out of here."

When we got close to Hooverville we heard four gunshots. We all spread into the woods and sneaked up to see what had happened. I peeked from behind a tree and could see a bunch of cops standing around with pistols out. All the men and boys and women that were left in Hooverville were bunched up on one side and the cops were on the other.

The fire had been lit and was burning bigger than ever, but now it was burning because the cops were tearing all of the shacks down and were throwing the wood and cardboard and hunks of cloth into the middle of it.

One of the cops dragged the big clothes-washing pot

over to the side and stuck his pistol down in it and shot four more times. Whew, instead of shooting people they were shooting holes into all of the pots and pans.

A man was yelling, "You yellow-belly lowlifes, you waited till you knew most of the men was gone, you cowards!"

The cops wouldn't talk or nothing, they just kept piling Flint's Hooverville into the fire.

I tried to see if I could spot Deza Malone but there were too many people.

It seemed like the only good thing that came out of going to Hooverville was that I finally kissed a girl. Maybe someone was trying to tell me something, what with me missing the train and the blue flyer floating back to me, maybe Deza Malone was right.

Maybe I should stay here in Flint.

I walked back farther into the woods and sat down. I pulled the blue flyer out of my pocket and opened my suitcase back up. I smoothed the flyer out and took another good look at it.

Maybe it came floating right back to me because this Herman E. Calloway really was my father. Wait a minute! I sat up. The names Caldwell and Calloway are a lot alike, both of them have eight letters and there aren't too many names that have a *C,* a *A,* a *L,* and a *W* all together like that. I remembered what I read in that Little-Big Book, *Gangbusters.* It said a good criminal chooses a alias that's kind of close to their own name. Except I couldn't figure out who was a criminal here and why anybody needed a alias.

I wanted to stay and look for Deza and her mother but it was too hard to hear all the people crying and arguing. Besides, I was still on the lam. I started walking.

If I hurried I could get breakfast at the mission.

# CHAPTER 9

*I GOT TO THE FOOD* line in plenty of time, but my pretend family wasn't anywhere around. I had to eat by myself, without the brown sugar.

After I was through I went back to the library and sat under my tree to wait for it to open. I couldn't stop thinking about Deza Malone and her dimple. How could her father find them now?

Finally I saw people going into the library.

The same librarian was there again. I said, "Good morning, ma'am."

"Good morning, young man."

"Could I please borrow a pencil and a piece of paper and see that book about how far one city is from another again, ma'am?"

She said, "Of course you may. You know, after I went home last night I finally recognized you. Didn't you and your mother used to come in here a long time ago?"

"Yes, ma'am."

She said, "And if I remember correctly you and your mother had quite different tastes in books. I remember your mother used to like mysteries and fairy tales, isn't that so?"

Man, I can't believe she remembered that!

"And you're the little fellow who used to come in all the time and ask Miss Hill for books about the Civil War, aren't you?"

"Yes, ma'am."

She said, "I thought so!" She handed me the pencil and paper and the cities book, then said, "And when you're done with the book bring it back and I have something special for you!" She had a huge smile on her face.

I said, "Thank you, ma'am," but I didn't get too excited 'cause I know the kind of things librarians think are special.

I went over to a table and found Flint and Grand Rapids in the lines of the book. I looked where the two lines met and it said 120. Wow! That was going to be a good little walk.

Next I wrote down 120, then divided it by 5, that came up to 24. That meant I'd have to walk for twenty-four hours to reach Grand Rapids, one whole day and one whole night.

I figured it would be easiest to do the night part first so I decided to stick around the library until it got dark, then head for Grand Rapids. I wrote down all the names of all the cities I'd have to pass through to get there, Owosso, Ovid, St. John's, Ionia and Lowell, and put the paper in my pocket.

When I took the cities book back the librarian was still smiling. She said, "I'll bet you've been dying to know what your surprise is, haven't you?"

I lied. "Yes, ma'am."

She reached under her desk and pulled out a thick, thick book called *The Pictorial History of the War Between the States*.

Wow! The book was gigantic!

"Thank you very much, ma'am!"

She said, "Enjoy, enjoy, enjoy!"

I took the book back to my table. I didn't want to tell her that I wasn't really interested in history, it was just that the best gory pictures in the world came from the Civil War. And this book was full of them. It really was a great book.

There's another thing that's strange about the library, it seems like time flies when you're in one. One second I was opening the first page of the book, hearing the cracking sound the pages make, smelling all the page powder, and reading what battle the picture on that page was from, and the next second the librarian was standing over me saying, "I am very impressed, you really devoured that book, didn't you? But it's time to close now, you may start up again first thing tomorrow!"

I couldn't believe it, it'd happened again! I'd spent the whole day reading. Her words snapped a spell that was on me, and my stomach started growling right away. I was going to be too late for the mission.

When she was walking me to the door the librarian stopped at her desk and said, "Now I know that knowledge is a food, but I couldn't help noticing you never went to eat. You must be very hungry."

She handed me a paper bag and gave me another smile.

"Thank you, ma'am!"

She smiled. "See you tomorrow."

I said, "Yes, ma'am. Thank you for everything."

I went back under the Christmas tree and got my suitcase. By this time tomorrow I'd be looking at the face of the man who had to be my father. I started eating the cheese sandwich the librarian gave me.

And then I headed out for Grand Rapids.


IT'S FUNNY HOW IDEAS ARE, in a lot of ways they're just like seeds. Both of them start real, real small and then . . .

woop, zoop, sloop . . . before you can say Jack Robinson they've gone and grown a lot bigger than you ever thought they could.

If you look at a great big maple tree it's hard to believe it started out as a little seed. I mean if you pick up one of those maple tree seeds and turn it over a couple of times in your hand there's no way your brain will buy that this little thing can grow up into something so big you have to bend your neck back just to see the top of it. Something so big that you can hang a swing on it, or build a tree house in it, or drive a car into it and kill yourself and any bad-lucked passengers that might be taking a ride with you.

Ideas are a lot like that, that's what the idea of Herman E. Calloway being my father started as, something so teeny that if I hadn't paid it no mind it would've blown away with the first good puff of wind. But now here it was so big and important and spread out.

The idea first got started when I was looking in my suitcase at one of the flyers showing Herman E. Calloway and his band. That was like the seed falling out of a tree and getting planted.

It started busting its head out of the dirt when me and the other boys at the Home were getting our nightly teasing from the biggest bully there, Billy Burns.

He'd said, "I don't even belong in this place. I been put here by mistake and it ain't going to be long before my momma comes and gets me out."

Bugs said, "Billy, how come it's taking your momma so long to find out where you're at? She must have a real bad rememory. Seems like since she was the one what dropped you off here she'd've remembered where she left you by now."

Billy said, "Well, well, well, will you take a look at who piped up, Mr. Bugs. You know, I've seen lots of people who have roach-infected houses, but you're the first person I've seen who's got a roach-infected head. I wouldn't expect a little ignorant roach-head like you to know nothing about folks coming back here to get you out, you don't even have no idea who your momma and daddy is. Any fool you see walking down the street could be them."

He looked at the rest of us and said, "Seven little boys in this room and not a one of y'all knows who your folks is. This is a sure-enough sad collection of souls here, boy."

I said, "That's not true, I know who my momma is, I lived with her for six years."

Another boy said, "Me too, I lived with my momma for a long time."

Billy Burns said to me, "Is that right? And what about your old man? How many years you live with him? I got a nickel here and you know what it says?"

Billy'd stole a nickel from somewhere and held it up so's the buffalo on it was looking out at us. He pretended the buffalo was talking, it had a deep voice like you'd figure a buffalo would. It said, "Billy, my man, go ahead and bet this little no-momma fool that he don't know who his daddy is, then I'd have another nickel to bang around in your pocket with."

Even before I had a chance to think I said, "You owe me a nickel, my daddy plays a giant fiddle and his name is Herman E. Calloway."

And with those words that I didn't even mean to say that little seed of a idea started growing.

The idea got bigger and stronger when I'd sit up at night and wonder why Momma'd kept those flyers. It dug its roots in deep and started spreading out when I got old enough to understand that Momma must've known she wasn't going to be around too long and was trying to leave me a message about who my daddy was and why she couldn't never talk about him. I knew Momma must be too embarrassed about why he wasn't with us and was trying to break it to me gentle. The only trouble was she waited too long.

I mean what other reason could there be for Momma to keep all these things I have in my suitcase and treat them like they were treasures, and why did I know way down in my guts that they were real, real important, so important that I didn't feel comfortable unless I knew where they were all the time?

That little idea had gone and sneaked itself into being a mighty maple, tall enough that if I looked up at the top of it I'd get a crick in my neck, big enough for me to hang a climbing rope in, strong enough that I made up my mind to walk clean across the state of Michigan.

I opened my suitcase and pulled the flyers out before it got dark. I put the blue one with the writing about Flint on it on the bottom and looked at the others. Two of them had the same picture of Herman E. Calloway and the two guys but the first was called "Herman E. Calloway and the Terminally Unhappy Blues Band," they were called "Masters of the Delta Blues," and the other one was called "Herman E. Calloway and the Gifted Gents of Gospel—Featuring Miss Grace 'Blessed' Thomas's Vocals," they were the "Servants of the Master's Salvation."

The two other flyers just had little drawings. The first one was a drawing of a accordion and told about a band named "H. E. Callowski and the Wonderful Warblers of Warsaw," who were the "Masters of the Polka." The second one was of a picture of some mountains and it told about a band named "H. E. Bonnegut and the Boisterous Big Band of Berlin," who were the "Masters of All We Behold."

I put the flyers back in the suitcase and stood up. Just like Bugs, I was going west!

# CHAPTER 10

*FLINT ENDED* all of a sudden and I was in the country. It was like one of those days that it's raining on one side of the street and not on the other. Here you have Flint and a sidewalk, you take one baby step, and here you have country and a dirt path. On the sidewalk side a sign said, YOU ARE NOW LEAVING FLINT, HURRY BACK, and on the dirt path side, YOU ARE NOW ENTERING FLINT — ENJOY YOUR STAY.

I jumped in and out of Flint around seven times before that got boring and I decided I'd better head for Grand Rapids. It was already very, very dark and unless things were different in the country it wasn't going to be getting light anytime soon.

One hundred and twenty miles. It didn't take too much time before I figured out that twenty-four hours' worth of walking was a lot longer than I thought it would be. I must've only been walking for a couple of minutes when everything changed.

First off there were the sounds. Flint could be pretty noisy, what with cars honking horns and trucks with no mufflers on them shifting gears and people yelling out at each other so you couldn't tell if they were happy or about to bust out fighting.

Out here in the country the sounds were loud too, but what I was hearing was the sound of bugs and toady-frogs and mice and rats playing a dangerous, scary kind of hide-and-go-seek where they rustle around and try to keep away from each other or try to find each other. Instead of being tagged and called "it" like the way human beans play the game, out here the ones that got got, got ate up. Every step I took toward Grand Rapids I could hear the sounds of mouse bones and bug skeletons being busted up by the teeth of bigger things.

Every once in a while a couple of cats would give out the kind of howls and yowls that would make the hair on your neck jump up if you were a human bean and your heart turn into a little cup of shaky yellow custard if you were a mouse.

I walked and walked and walked. Some of the time a car would come by and I'd have to duck into the bushes and wait till it had passed, so I don't think I was doing any five miles a hour.

I felt like I'd been walking all night but I'd only gone through three little towns.

I was getting so tired that I started to forget to duck in the bushes when a car would roar by. Some of the time they'd see me and step on their brakes for a second, then speed off. Most times they never noticed me.

Another car bounced over the top of a hill. The lights blinded me for a second and then I ducked into the bushes again.

The guy in the car stepped on the brakes to slow down and I could see him twist his neck around.

He stuck the car in reverse and pulled to a stop about thirty giant steps away from where I was hiding. His door opened and he stepped out and started walking slow toward my bushes. He brushed his hand over his head and put on a black hat like the kind the police or some army men wear. But all the cops I'd ever seen were white so I knew this guy must be a soldier.

He stopped and put his fingers to his lips and whistled. The whistle was so loud that it made me duck down and put my hands over my ears, it felt like he'd blown it right inside my head. All the bugs and toady-frogs shut right up, they quit chasing and biting each other 'cause this had to be the loudest whistle they'd ever heard too.

Rocks were crunching as the man in the black hat walked a couple of steps up the road, then stopped again. For the second time he blasted my ears with that whistle. The noise-making critters in that patch of road got quiet.

He said, "Say hey!"

He waited, then yelled, "Say hey! I know my eyes aren't what they used to be, but I know they aren't so bad that they'd lie to me about seeing a young brown-skinned boy walking along the road just outside of Owosso, Michigan, at two-thirty in the morning."

I couldn't tell if he was talking to me or to hisself. I peeked up to see if I could get a better look at this man. He came closer to me, then stopped about ten giant steps away.

"And I'ma tell you, I've seen some things out of place before and a young brown-skinned boy walking along the road just outside of Owosso, Michigan, at two-thirty in the morning is definitely not where he ought to be. In fact, what is definite is that neither one of us should be out here this time of night."

He squatted down and said, "Are you still there?"

I raised my head a little higher to get a better look at him and his big car. He'd left the door open and I could hear the engine of the car grumbling, it was saying, *wugga, wugga, wugga, wugga, wugga.*

"Son," he said, "this is no time to play. I don't know and I don't care why you're out here, but let me tell you I know you're a long way from home. Are you from Flint?"

How could he tell I was from Flint just by seeing my face for a second in his headlights? I wonder how grown folks know so doggone much just by looking at you.

Something was telling me to answer him but I still wanted to get a better look.

He stood up. "You know what? I bet if I can't get you to come out with talk I got something else that might make you show your face.

"From the quick look I got at you, you seemed a little on the puny side. I'll bet anything you're hungry. Just so happens that I've got a spare baloney and mustard sandwich and an apple in the car. You interested?"

Shucks. How did he know I was so hungry?

Then he said, "Might even have some extra red pop."

Before my brain could stop it my stomach made my mouth yell out, "But I don't like mustard, sir."

The man could tell which bushes I was hiding in but

he didn't bum-rush them or try to get me, he just laughed and said, "Well, I didn't check, but I don't suppose the mustard's been glued on, I'll bet you we can scrape it off. What do you say?"

I was carefuller talking to him this time so he couldn't track where I was. I turned my head and talked sideways out of my mouth like one of those ventriloquists. "Just leave them at the side of the road and I'll get them. And please open the bottle of pop, sir, I don't have a bottle key on me."

He squatted back down again and said, "Oh, no, can't do that. The deal is I feed you, you show me your face."

From the way the man talked he seemed like he was OK and before my brain could stop it my stomach told the rest of me to slide my suitcase deeper into the weeds and walk out.

The man stayed squatted down and said, "I knew I saw something. A deal's a deal so I'ma go get your food, all right?"

"Yes, sir."

He stood up, turned his back to me, then ducked inside the car. A second later he came back with a brown paper bag and a big bottle of red pop.

"Here it is."

He stood there acting like I was going to have to come over to him and get it.

"Could you put them down and I'll eat them and you can keep driving, sir?"

He laughed again. "Thanks for your concern, but I've got a little time to spare."

With him standing there in the dark dangling the bottle of red pop out of his right hand and the red taillights of the car behind him shining through the bottle it looked like the reddest red in the world. I walked right up to the man like I was hypnotized. I forgot all my manners and reached right out.

He raised the bottle over his head. "Hold on now."

"Could I have some of the pop, sir?"

He smiled. "That's not why I said hold on, I said it because we have some talking to do first."

My eyes left the bottle and looked at the man.

His hat wasn't a cop hat or a soldier hat, it was the kind of cap men wore who drive fancy cars for rich folks. And it wasn't black, it was red.

He said, "I've got a problem and I need you to help me figure it out."

Uh-oh. What he'd just said is another one of Bud Caldwell's Rules and Things for Having a Funner Life and Making a Better Liar Out of Yourself. This was Number 87.

### RULES AND THINGS NUMBER 87

**When a Adult Tells You They Need Your Help
with a Problem Get Ready to Be Tricked—**

### Most Times This Means They Just Want You to
### Go Fetch Something for Them.

The man said, "My problem is I'm not quite as brave as you are. I'm feeling very, very uncomfortable standing on the side of the road just outside of Owosso, Michigan, at two-thirty in the morning, and the sooner you can put my mind at ease about what you're doing out here the sooner we both can go about our business, OK?"

I nodded.

He waited a second, then nodded too.

I nodded back.

He said, "Well?"

I was too doggone tired and hungry to think up a good lie. "Nothing, sir."

He looked disappointed. "What's your name, son?"

"Bud, not Buddy, sir."

"Now there's an unusual name. Did you run away from home, Bud-not-Buddy?"

I could tell this guy was poking fun at me but I answered anyway. "Yes, sir."

"OK, that's a start."

He handed me the bottle of red pop. He must've had it sitting in ice in the car, it was cold and sweet and delicious.

After a couple of seconds he pulled the bottle away from my mouth.

"Hold on, hold on, don't belt it all down on the first pull. There's plenty here."

I slowed way down.

"OK, Bud, you've run away from home, where is that?"

I don't know if it was because of the red pop juicing up my brain or because I'm such a good liar, but one of those things got me thinking again real quick.

The first thing I knew was that no matter what I told him this man wasn't going to let me stay out here by myself, but the nervous way he kept looking around was making things seem so scary that not staying out here was OK.

The second thing I knew was that I couldn't tell this man about the Home or the Amoses. I wasn't about to let him take me back to either one of them.

The man said, "Where's home, Bud?"

Then another jolt of red pop must've pumped through my heart because my brain came up with a perfect lie.

"I ran away from Grand Rapids, sir."

See how perfect the lie was? Maybe this guy would feel sorry for me and put me on a bus to Grand Rapids and I wouldn't have to do any more doggone walking. He must have some money, anyone driving a car like this would have to be rich or at least know somebody who was rich.

The man scratched under the back of his hat and said, "Grand Rapids!" He said that like it was the most unbelievable thing in the world, like you'd need to put six exclamation points after it.

Something about the way he said it made me nervous but I answered him. "Yes, sir." That's the bad thing about lying, once you say one you've usually got to stick with it.

"Well I'll be . . . ," the man said. "That's where I'm from, I left there not an hour and a half ago."

He snatched the bottle out of my hand, grabbed my arm, walked me over to the passenger's side of the car and started to open the door.

I was glad I was going to be getting a ride but I said, "Sir, I left my suitcase over in the bushes, can we please get it?"

"See, my eyes aren't near as bad as I thought they were, I knew you had a box or something. Bud-not-Buddy, you don't know how lucky you are I came through here, some of these Owosso folks used to have a sign hanging along here that said, and I'm going to clean up the language for you, it said, 'To Our Negro Friends Who Are Passing Through, Kindly Don't Let the Sun Set on Your Rear End in Owosso!' "

He must not have trusted me 'cause he kept holt of my arm. We went over to the bushes and I grabbed my suitcase. Then he walked me back to the car.

When he opened the passenger's side door I could see that there was a big box sitting on the front seat. The man never let go of my arm and wrestled the box over into the backseat.

If he would've let go of my arm for just one second I would've run like the devil was chasing me. On the side of the box some big red letters said as clear as anything, URGENT: CONTAINS HUMAN BLOOD!!!

Oh, man, here we go again!

My heart started jumping around in my stomach. The only kind of people who would carry human blood around in a car were vampires! They must drink it if they were taking a long trip and couldn't find any people to get blood from. This guy figured he'd rather have my fresh blood than blood out of a bottle!

I barely heard him say, "Get in. I'm going back to Grand Rapids tomorrow, I'll send a telegram to your folks and then take you back."

Then he made his first mistake, he let go of my arm. I slid into the car and he closed the door behind me. Quick as anything I locked the door and crawled over to the driver's side of the car and pulled that door closed and locked it just as the vampire reached for the handle to get in. I dug around in my pocket and pulled my knife out and put it under my leg.

I put my hands on the steering wheel and looked at the gearshift to try to figure which way was "Go." I stretched my legs out as far as they'd reach and could just get to the gas pedal.

I pulled the gear lever down and the car took off with the vampire running as hard as he could to catch me.

Wow! If I kept things like this up I would knock Baby Face Nelson off the FBI's ten most wanted list!

# CHAPTER 11

*THE CAR ONLY WENT* thirty giant steps before it commenced to bucking and finally cut right off. The vampire guy finally caught up with me. He was looking very surprised, he just tapped on the window with his knuckle. He said, "Roll the window down for a minute, Bud."

Sometimes it's terrible to have been brought up proper. I couldn't help myself, I rolled the window down just enough so that our words could get in and out but his hand or claws couldn't.

He said, "OK, what's this?"

I said, "Don't you think I can read? How come you're carrying real human blood around in your car?" I showed him my jackknife. "I'ma warn you, I know how to kill vampires. This knife is genuine solid twenty-four-karat silver."

He put both of his hands over his face and shook his head back and forth a couple of times. He said, "Sweet baby Jesus, why me?"

Then he said, "Bud, if you were from Flint I might think you believe that, but you're a Grand Rapids boy, you've got to be smarter than that. If I was a vampire why have I got that sandwich and bottle of red pop?"

I thought for a second, then the answer jumped out. "Bait!"

He put his hands back over his face. This time when he pulled them away he was laughing. He said, "Bud, if I was a vampire I wouldn't have to catch little boys, I'd just stick my fangs into one of those bottles and have my supper. Besides, where've you ever heard of a vampire that knew how to drive a car?"

That made sense, in all the moving picture shows I'd seen and all the books I'd read about vampires I never could think of seeing one that could drive a car. But I wasn't going to take any chances.

"Could I please see your teeth, sir?"

"What?"

"Your teeth, sir."

The man mumbled something, shook his head again, then leaned close to the window glass and opened his mouth.

Even though he didn't have fangs his teeth still looked kinda scary. They looked like they could bite a pretty good grapefruit-sized chunk out of you.

Then he said, "Bud, I've got to get this blood to Hurley Hospital in Flint, they need it right away for someone's operation. I can look at you and tell you're far too smart to believe in any nonsense like vampires, son. Be a good boy and open the door."

I pulled the lock up for him and scooted over to the passenger's side of the car. I unlocked my door just in case he had any tricks up his sleeve.

He got in the car and said, "You'll never know how grateful I am to you, Bud. I'll take that horrible image of you putting the car in gear to drive away while I stood by the side of the road in Owosso, Michigan, at two-thirty in the morning to my grave with me. Thank God you don't know how to drive."

"No, sir, but if you'da showed me some fangs I'da learned real quick."

Just in case, I watched the way he put the car in gear so's the next time something like this happened I'd know how to make a clean getaway. Me and the man headed back toward Flint, driving over the same road it took me so long to walk. Going like this I wasn't never going to get away from this doggone city.

We hadn't been driving for a minute before he started asking a whole slew of questions. Questions that I had to be very careful about giving the right answers to.

He said, "Don't you feel bad about worrying your mother like this, Bud-not-Buddy?"

"My mother is dead, sir." Most times if you tell a adult that they'll leave you alone, but not this man.

"What? I'm sorry to hear that, Bud. So you stay with your daddy?"

"Yes, sir."

"Right in Grand Rapids?"

"Yes, sir."

"What's his name, does he work for the railroad?"

"No, sir." The seed started sticking its head out further and further. "His name is Herman E. Calloway and he plays the biggest doggone fiddle you'll ever see."

The man shouted, "What?"

I said, "Really, sir, I swear 'fore God it's the biggest fiddle in the world."

He said, "I know your father, everybody in Grand Rapids does."

I didn't say anything.

He said, "Well, I'll be. You know, at first glimpse I wouldn't say you look that much like Herman, but now that I look at you I suppose you do. Of course he's quite a bit bigger, if you know what I mean."

This was the best news I'd had all day, my face nearly

split in half from my giant smile. "Yes, sir, folks say I'm the spitting image of my old man."

He really started shooting the questions at me so to stop him I said, "Sir, could I please have the sandwich and the rest of the red pop before I answer any more questions?"

He slapped his forehead and said, "Oh, I'm sorry, Bud, I was so surprised about who you are and so happy that you didn't drive off that I forgot all about our deal."

He handed me the sandwich and the pop and the apple. I was so hungry that I forgot all about scraping the mustard off the baloney sandwich and even like that it was the best sandwich I'd ever had in my life.

"Bud," he said, "my name's Mr. Lewis. Now if you were about fifteen, twenty years older you could call me Lefty. But you're not, so you can't. Mr. Lewis will do just fine."

I shoved the part of the sandwich that I was chewing into the side of my mouth so I could say, "Yes, sir, Mr. Lewis, sir."

He said, "I'm not ashamed to admit it, you gave me a scare here tonight that I'll never forget. I just know I'll be having nightmares about meeting you for the rest of my life. I'll wake up in a cold sweat many a night with the picture of you and my car pulling away with that blood on the seat.

"I can see it all now, I'll be sound asleep, deep in the middle of a Ruth Dandridge dream, when all of a sudden I'll be standing on the side of the road in Owosso, Michigan, at two-thirty in the morning and I'll be seeing my car and that blood pulling away with nothing of you showing but that little peanut-head of yours peeking up over the dash."

He looked at me out of the side of his eye.

"Anyone ever tell you you've got a little peanut-head?"

I glugged down the pop I'd been swishing around in my mouth and said, "No, sir."

"Well," he said, "this may be the first time but unless you undergo some major surgery I'll bet it won't be the last."

"Yes, sir."

He waited a second, then sounded kind of disappointed when he said, "Don't take it so seriously, Bud, I am teasing, you know."

I started in on the apple. "Yes, sir."

"Ever been in the army, Bud?"

"No, sir."

"Well, I've got to tell you, I haven't heard so many 'sirs' since I was back at Fort Gordon in Georgia training for the Big War."

I almost said, "Yes, sir," but I looked at him and guessed he was still teasing.

I took another drink of the red pop and saw that when I was raising the bottle I'd accidentally let some of the sandwich slip out of my mouth down into the pop. There were a couple of chunks of chewed-up bread, a blob of baloney and some of the mustard swimming around in the bottle. The mustard was real pretty, it looked like some kind of magical fog, every time I moved the bottle the mustardy smoke went into a different kind of shape.

Lefty Lewis said, "How about sharing that pop, Bud?"

Uh-oh. He took one look and handed it back.

He said, "Nothing personal, Bud, I've raised three kids and have two grandkids, I've learned the hard way about drinking after young folks. But I do believe you need to get in and see a doctor soon, son, it looks to me like you've got a serious backwash problem, that's the most food I've ever seen floating around in a bottle of pop. In fact, that doesn't look like red pop anymore, it looks more like red stew."

I real quick chugged the rest of the pop down and ate the apple real slow because I figured as soon as I was done with it the questions would start up again.

Lefty Lewis said, "Aren't you sleepy?"

This was perfect! I could pretend I was falling asleep and then come up with some answers that would get me to Grand Rapids for sure. I yawned real big. "A little bit, sir."

"All right, here, give me that core, I think the only thing that's left is a seed or two anyway."

I handed him the apple core and he put it and the wax paper from the sandwich in the paper bag.

"You just stretch out there and have some sleep. In

about an hour you'll be in a nice comfortable bed. We can have our talk in the morning."

He reached in the backseat and said, "Here," and handed me a jacket. "You can use this for a blanket."

The jacket smelled real good, like spice and soap.

Lefty Lewis said, "Oh, Bud-not-Buddy, one more thing before you doze off. Could you reach over into that box and hand me one of those bottles of blood? I haven't had a bite to eat all day."

I kept my eyes closed and smiled. I knew I was going to be safe, because I'd never heard of a vampire that could drive a car and I'd never seen one that had such a good sense of humor. Besides, I kept my jackknife open under my leg and he looked like he'd believed me when I told him it was made out of real silver, even though it probably wasn't.

As soon as I had the jacket over me the smell of the spice and soap and the sound of the crickets and toady-frogs outside made my eyes get real heavy.


Wow! I must have been real, real tired. Walking and ducking in and out of the bushes between Flint and Owosso was a lot more work than I thought it was.

Most of the time since Momma died, if someone even walks close to where I'm sleeping I'm up in a flash, my eyes fly open and I'm looking right at them. At one of the foster houses where I'd stayed a woman told me she knew I was going to be a criminal because "anyone who sleeps that light has got to have a guilty conscience." Most of the time the sound of someone else going from sleep breathing to awake breathing in the same room as me is enough to get me up.

But this morning I felt like I was at the bottom of a well that someone had filled with tons of thick chocolate pudding. Someone was calling my name from way up at the top of the well. She was saying, "Bud. Bud. Bud."

Waves from the pudding were slogging me back and forth, back and forth.

"Bud. Wake up, Bud." It was a woman's voice and her hands were trying to shake me awake. Uh-oh. This is Number 29 of my rules:

### RULES AND THINGS NUMBER 29

**When You Wake Up and Don't Know for Sure
Where You're At and There's a Bunch of
People Standing Around You, It's Best to Pretend
You're Still Asleep Until You Can Figure
Out What's Going On and What You Should Do.**

I kept my eyes closed, acting like I was out cold.

The woman said, "Poppa, what on earth are all these lumps and bites on this baby's face?"

A man answered, "Well, he was walking all the way

from Grand Rapids to Flint, it looks like he provided a pretty paltry meal for every mosquito on the way."

The woman said, "This poor child must be dead, I hate getting him up. I wish he could stay with us for a while, at least until he's had his sleep."

Then I remembered who I was with because Lefty Lewis said, "I know, but I've got to get back. He can sleep in the car on the way back to Grand Rapids."

The woman rolled back the blanket they'd put over me and said, "Poppa, look at his legs, this boy's as skinny as a rail."

Shucks, they'd taken off my knickers when they put me in this bed. Now I was going to have to pretend I was asleep even longer, at least until I could figure a way out of being so embarrassed.

Lefty Lewis said, "Yeah, he's puny. Good thing his legs don't touch when he walks 'cause if those two twigs got to rubbing against one another he'd have a fire going in no time."

The woman said, "That's not funny. He doesn't look like he's been fed right. Now who's his father again, you said you know him?"

"Everyone in Grand Rapids does, I'm surprised you can't remember him. He's quite a big fish there."

See! I told you it was smart to pretend you were asleep some of the time. Now I was going to learn some things about my father.

The woman said, "What kind of man is he that he let this child be so thin? And look at the condition of the boy's clothes. Everything is either too small for him or almost in tatters. Where is this child's mother? There's not much of a woman's touch about him."

Lefty Lewis said, "It seems to me that the Mrs. Calloway I knew passed a long time ago. The boy says he's ten and I'm sure she died quite a while before that. But you know how musicians are, there must be at least a few Mrs. Calloways I don't know anything about."

That meant that my dad was married to someone before he married my mom.

Lefty Lewis's daughter said, "Well, I think it's a sin. I'm of half a mind to keep this boy for a while to put some fear in his daddy's heart. But he probably wouldn't even miss him."

Lefty Lewis said, "Now you stop being so judgmental, Herman's got a reputation for being no-nonsense, not mean."

"Does this child have any brothers or sisters?"

"I believe he's got a sister, but she'd have to be his half-sister, she must be full-grown by now."

The woman pulled the blanket back over my legs and shook me again. I was glad I could stop pretending I was asleep, I was sick and tired of hearing about how skinny I am and what a mixed-up family I come from. She said real soft, "Bud, wake up. Come on, sweetie, I've got a nice breakfast waiting for you."

Food! I started blinking and acting like those were the first words I'd heard that morning. I said, "Huh?" like I was kind of confused.

The woman smiled real big and said, "Oh-ho, I see that got your attention, didn't it? Good morning, young man."

"Good morning, ma'am. Good morning, Mr. Lewis."

He said, "Hey, you remembered my name, I'm impressed. Good morning, Walking Willie. We've got to hit the road in a bit, better hurry up and get some food in your belly."

He acted like he was whispering just to me when he said, "The food in this joint ain't the best, but I guarantee after you eat here you won't be hungry for days, this meal's going to be sitting on your stomach like a rock for a good long time."

The woman said, "Ignore him, Bud. My father doesn't mean anything, he just can't stop teasing."

I said, "I know, ma'am, he told me I've got a head shaped like a peanut."

The woman slapped her father on the arm. "Poppa! I can't believe you've teased this child already. What is on your mind?"

Lefty Lewis rubbed his hand over my head and said, "Look at this noggin, I rest my case. Boy looks like one of George Washington Carver's experiments sprouted legs and run off. You sure you're not from Tuskegee, Alabama, Bud?"

I said, "No, sir."

The woman sucked in her lower lip and swallowed a smile before she said, "See, Bud, he can't help himself. But he really doesn't mean anything, do you, Poppa?"

The way she asked that you'd have to be pretty stupid not to know how to answer her. Lefty Lewis said, "Not a thing. It's just that you—"

His daughter spoke up. "My name is Mrs. Sleet, Bud."

"Pleased to meet you, ma'am."

"Now, while you wash up I'm going to go get some clothes that my boy outgrew a while ago, barely been used. So when you get dressed you come on down and we'll eat, you chose a great day to visit, we're having a very special breakfast today—pancakes, sausages and toast and a big glass of orange juice. You can meet Scott and Kim, too. How's that sound?"

"That sounds real good, ma'am. Thank you very much."

"Don't mention it, it's a pleasure to have such a well-mannered young visitor."

Mrs. Sleet and Lefty Lewis left the room. As soon as they were a little bit down the hall I could hear her start in on scolding her father again.

"I just can't believe it. You know, Momma was right about you. . . ."

All I could hear next was him mumbling some answer, then her slapping his arm again.

After I got out of the bathroom, I saw that Mrs. Sleet had put some clean clothes on the bed. My old clothes were gone, all except for my drawers which I hadn't taken off. She'd even put clean drawers out for me so when I put them on I stuck my old ones down in the pocket of my new pants. I could ditch them when I got to Grand Rapids. It's too embarrassing to have strangers look at your dirty drawers, even if the stranger is as nice as Mrs. Sleet.

The new clothes were just a little bit too big, but they were long pants and not knickers so I didn't care, I rolled cuffs into the pants and sleeves and they fit pretty doggone good.

Man, my first pair of trousers!

I let my nose lead me down to where the smell of pancakes and toast was coming from. The Sleets had a room for eating and it had a great big table right in the middle of it. The first thing I noticed was a huge pile of pancakes sitting on a blue and white plate on top of the table.

Lefty Lewis was sitting with Mrs. Sleet's kids. The little girl had a big smile and the boy was looking at me kind of hard. It wasn't one of those put-up-your-dukes looks, it was just a look like one dog gives another dog that might be passing through his neighborhood.

Lefty Lewis said, "Bud, these two worrisome midgets are my favorite grandkids. Kim is my favorite granddaughter and Scott is my favorite grandson. Of course they're my only grandkids, so in fairness you'd have to say they're also my least favorite grandkids."

These two kids had had a lot of practice being around their teasing old granddad because they didn't pay him no mind at all.

I said, "Hi, my name is Bud, not Buddy."

The little girl said, "That's a strange name, Bud-not-Buddy," and even though she was kind of young and scrawny to be teasing folks I could tell that that was exactly what she was doing.

Lefty Lewis laughed and said, "That's my girl," then he went into the kitchen.

Scott looked up to make sure the grown folks weren't around and said, "You really run away from home?"

I had to stop and think, it's one thing to lie to a grown-up, most times adults want to hear something that lets them take their attention off you and put it on something else. That makes it easy and not too bad to lie to them. You're really just giving them what they want.

It's different when you lie to another kid. Most times kids really do want to know what they're asking you.

I guess I'd been thinking too long 'cause he said, "You run all the way from Grand Rapids to Owosso? Was it 'cause your daddy use to beat you?"

I could answer that with the swear-'fore-God truth. "Shucks, my daddy never laid a hand on me in his life."

"Then how come you run?"

"I didn't like where I was." That wasn't a lie.

"Well, if you're lying about your daddy beating you, you better scram right after breakfast 'cause my gramps is taking you straight back home."

"My daddy never laid a hand on me."

The little girl said, "Scott, you talk too much, let him sit down." Then she told me, "Momma's gonna be bringing the sausages in in a minute, you like sausages?"

"Uh-huh." I'd never had sausages before but if that was what was making the house smell so good I was going to love it.

Kim said, "Good, 'cause my grampa brought them all the way from Grand Rapids. He always brings us good food and we're going to share it with you 'cause Momma says you're our special guest and we have to treat you nice. Am I being nice?"

"So far."

"Good. I'll make a deal with you."

Uh-oh. "What kind of a deal?"

"I'll sing a song that I made up all by myself and when I'm done I get to ask you one question and you have to answer and cross your heart you'll tell the truth."

This didn't sound too bad.

"OK."

"Here goes, it took me a very long time to make this song up, so I hope you like it."

The boy said, "Oh, brother."

Kim sang,

> *"Mommy says no*
> *Mommy says no,*
> *I listen, you don't,*
> *Wha-ha-ha-ha.*
> *The building falls down,*
> *The building falls down,*
> *You get crushed, I don't,*
> *Wha-ha-ha-ha."*

Boy. That was about the worst song I'd ever heard. Kim stood up and bowed like a princess.

I clapped my hands together kind of soft under the table.

She said, "Thank you very much."

Scott just shook his head.

Kim said, "OK, that's my part of the deal, now you've got to keep your part and answer any question I ask."

"OK."

"Now you can tell me all about how your mother died."

Scott's foot kicked at her under the table.

I said, "Who told you my momma died?"

The little girl said, "Oops," and stuffed something from her hand into her mouth.

"My momma got sick. She died real fast. She didn't feel no pain or no suffering."

Kim said, "I hope my mother never dies."

Scott said, "Stupid, everybody's got to die."

Kim said, "Ooh, I'm telling Momma you called me stupid."

He said, "You do and I'll tell her that you've got one of those pancakes in the pocket of your dress."

She shut right up.

I told her, "He's right, everybody's got to die. It's not sad unless they do it real slow and suffer. My momma died so quick and painless that she didn't even have time to close her eyes, she didn't even have time to make a face like she was hurting."

Both of Lefty Lewis's grandkids looked real surprised at this news.

Mrs. Sleet came into the room with another blue plate, covered with little round pieces of meat. Those had to be the sausages.

She saw the way her kids were looking at me with their mouths half opened and said, "Now you two aren't talking Bud's ear off, are you?"

Scott said, "No, Momma, I'm not, but Kim's coming real close to."

Kim said, "I was not, I was just making pleasant conversation."

Mrs. Sleet laughed and set the plate on the table right in front of me.

Lefty Lewis came out with a big glass jug filled with orange juice and sat down next to me.

Mrs. Sleet sat down and said, "Scott and Kim, would you say the grace, please?"

Everyone ducked their heads down and the two kids said,

> *"God is great,*
> *God is good,*
> *Let us thank him*
> *For our food.*
> *Amen."*

Then people started passing the big blue plates around and stabbing toast and pancakes and sausages with their forks. I watched to see how much everyone took and tried to take the same. Then I started to watch how much food the two kids put on their fork every time so I wouldn't look like a pig.

Lefty Lewis noticed I was taking a long time and told his daughter, "See what I told you, Nina, poor Bud-not-Buddy is so skinny and his stomach has shrunk down so much that just smelling the food has got the boy full. Oh, well, I guess that just means more food for the rest of us." Everyone except for me and Mrs. Sleet yelled a big cheer.

Eating with the Sleets and Lefty Lewis was really hard to do, not because they had bad table manners or nothing, but because they talked through the whole breakfast. And they kept trying to get me to talk too.

At the Home after grace was said we weren't allowed to say boo. Eating and being quiet is a hard habit to break. Every time one of these Sleets would talk to me and look at me like they expected a answer I'd look around first to make sure no one was watching. At the Home if you got caught talking during mealtime you'd have to get up and leave your food. If these Sleets had to live under those rules they'd all starve to death.

They talked after every swallow, they talked after every drink they took, they talked whilst they were wiping off their lips. Shucks, the little girl, Kim, talked with milk running down her throat, some of the time her words got gluggled up in what she was swallowing. And they laughed. Man, did they laugh.

It was hard to tell whose story they were laughing at, they were doing so much chattering.

Lefty Lewis was talking about radio shows and Scott was talking about going to a baseball game to watch Lefty Lewis pitch and Kim was talking about a little girl she didn't like and Mrs. Sleet was talking about some people called redcaps.

Kim said to her mother, "Mommy, can't you tell that Bud-not-Buddy doesn't know what a redcap is, you gotta explain better."

Mrs. Sleet said, "Oh, sorry, Bud, redcaps are the men who work at the railroad station loading the trains and taking people's bags to their cars. That's what Mr. Lewis does. My husband is a Pullman porter, he takes care of the people once they're on the trains."

Kim said, "Yeah, our dad gets to travel all over the country on trains for free!"

Scott said, "That's 'cause he's working, it's not for free, he gets paid to do it."

Lefty Lewis swallowed a big hunk of sausage and said, "And you know what, Bud? I bet the thing he misses most is Nina's cooking. I can't tell you how proud I am of how far my daughter's cooking has come. This might be hard to believe, but she used to be such a bad cook that her fried chicken was known to have turned a chicken hawk into a vegetarian."

Scott and Kim and Mrs. Sleet started busting a gut.

"Yup," Lefty Lewis said, "I brought a friend to Flint a couple of years ago and even though I'd warned him he tried to be polite and ate four of her pancakes. Pour soul held his stomach all the way back to Grand Rapids. Said to me, 'Lefty, I don't mean to show any disrespect, but those weren't pancakes your daughter served me, they were paincakes.' "

Mrs. Sleet laughed along with everyone else and said, "Well, I'm sure I don't need to hear any more of this," and picked up the empty sausage plate and went into the kitchen.

As soon as she got out of the room Kim whispered, "Quick, Grampa, tell Bud-not-Buddy how many times you had to pull the car over when you two were going back to Grand Rapids so that man could get out and vomick on the side of the road."

Before Lefty Lewis could answer, Mrs. Sleet came out of the kitchen with a big wooden spoon and whopped her father a good lick in the head.

# CHAPTER 12

*AFTER BREAKFAST* me and Mr. Lewis said goodbye to the Sleets and got back into the car. I leaned over the front seat to put my suitcase in the back.

"Mr. Lewis, someone stole all the blood last night!"

He said, "I'll say one thing for you, Bud, when you go to sleep you go way, way to sleep. You don't remember anything about last night after we got to Flint?"

I said, "I don't think so, sir."

"After you so rudely fell asleep on me we dropped the blood off at Hurley Hospital, then I gassed up, then I got in touch with your daddy to let him know you were all right."

Uh-oh. "What did he say, sir?"

"I didn't call him, I sent a telegram to the Log Cabin. He still owns that club, doesn't he?"

"Yes, sir."

"Good." Lefty Lewis leaned over and reached in the glove box of the car. He pulled out a flimsy piece of yellow paper and handed it to me.

Across the top of the paper it said in big letters, WESTERN UNION. Underneath that it said,

HEC STOP

BUD OK IN FLINT STOP AT 4309 NORTH ST

STOP RETURN 8PM WED STOP

LEFTY STOP

Man! I'll bet Herman E. Calloway was just as confused by this message as I was.

I said, "What does this mean, sir?"

Lefty Lewis said, "When you send a telegram the more letters you use the more money you have to pay, so you try to keep your messages as short as you can. Here, let me see it."

I handed him the paper.

He said, "OK, 'HEC,' that stands for your dad, Herman E. Calloway. 'Bud OK in Flint,' that lets him know how far you got and that you're safe. And you did get pretty far, Bud, maybe he won't be too hard on you when he sees how resourceful you were at running away. I know I'd've been darn proud of one of my kids if they'd've gotten that far, but I used to offer them money to run and they'd never take it.

" 'At 4309 North St,' that's my daughter's address. And 'Return 8PM Wed' lets him know I'm bringing you home by eight tonight."

I said, "What are all of those 'stops,' sir?"

He said, "That's the telegram office's way of saying 'period.' It just means that the sentence is over."

Lefty Lewis spent most of the day doing errands all around Flint. He made me promise to wait in the car for him. I was good and happy when he said, "That's it, Bud, time to head home."

We drove past that sign that said WELCOME TO FLINT on one side when he looked up and said, "Uh-oh."

Suddenly a sireen went off sounding like it was in the backseat of the car. I raised my head up to look over the seat out the back window. Uh-oh was right! There was a Flint police car right behind us with the red light on top of his roof flashing on and off, on and off, and with the sireen blasting. They'd found me!

Shucks, this doggone FBI was just as good as the movies said it was, they were just like those Royal Canadian Mountain Police, they always got their man! I crouched down as low as I could.

Lefty Lewis pulled the car over to the side of the road and said real calm and real slow, "Bud. It's very important that you listen very carefully to what I'm going to tell you and that you do exactly as I say." He kept his eyes stuck on the rearview mirror.

By the way he was acting I was starting to think that maybe Lefty Lewis was on the lam too. And wait a minute, how come this man didn't have a real name? Whoever heard of someone's momma naming him Lefty? That name had alias writ all over it!

Lefty sounds like a real good name for a stick-up man. It seemed like it would be real easy for Machine Gun Kelly to point at some poor slob and say, "That's the guy what ratted me out, Lefty. Finish him off!"

And what he just said about listening carefully and doing exactly what he said was Number 8 of Bud Caldwell's Rules and Things to Have a Funner Life and Make a Better Liar Out of Yourself.

### RULES AND THINGS NUMBER 8

**Whenever a Adult Tells You to Listen
Carefully and Talks to You in a Real Calm Voice Do
Not Listen, Run as Fast as You Can Because
Something Real Terrible Is Just Around the
Corner. Especially If the Cops Are Chasing You.**

I stared at Lefty Lewis, keeping my fingers crossed that the next thing he said wouldn't be "You'll never take us alive, copper!"

Instead, he said, "Bud, are you listening, Bud?"

I had to play along until I got a chance to make a break. I said, "Yes, sir."

"Attaboy. First close your mouth. Good. Now I want you to take the box that is next to me and quickly put it all the way beneath your seat."

I picked up a box that was about the size of a big thick book and slid it under my seat.

Lefty Lewis said, "Good boy. Now stay put and don't say anything." He winked at me and said, "Don't worry, it's all right."

He opened his door and walked back to the police car.

I tried to decide what to do. If I made a break for it I was sure the coppers would plug me, but maybe Lefty Lewis would rassle the gun away before they got a good shot off. Or maybe, just maybe Lefty Lewis would take a bullet for me.

OK, I told myself, I'ma count to ten, then I'm going to reach into the backseat, snatch my suitcase and book out for those buildings.

One, two, three, four, five, six, seven, eight, nine, ten.

OK, I'm gonna count to ten again.

One, two, three, four, five, six, seven, eight, nine, ten.

OK, this time I'm really, *really* going to grab that doggone . . . The cop and Lefty Lewis were standing at the door. The cop said, "I want to take a look in the trunk."

Him and Mr. Lewis went around to the back and the

trunk opened and I heard someone rumbling around in it. I heard a loud bang and nearly jumped out of my seat.

Whew! It was only Mr. Lewis closing the trunk. They walked back to the driver's door.

The policeman looked in the backseat and said, "What's in the suitcase?"

Mr. Lewis said, "Those are Bud's things. He was visiting here in Flint and I'm taking him home to Grand Rapids."

The policeman looked at me and said, "Oh. Your grandson, huh? You two look just alike."

Lefty Lewis said, "Why, thank you, Officer, I always thought the boy was unusually handsome."

The cop didn't have a good sense of humor, he said, "All right, you're free to go. We can't be too careful, I don't know if you've heard, but we're having a lot of trouble in the factories here. We've been stopping all cars we don't recognize. There've been reports that some more of those stinking labor organizers might be sneaking up here from Detroit."

Mr. Lewis said, "You don't say."

The cop said, "Drive carefully," and he touched the brim of his cop hat the way a cowboy in the moving pictures does.

Lefty Lewis got in the car, started it and we pulled back out on the highway.

He made a scary face at me and said, "Bud, this has really been a couple of lucky days for you. First I save you from being eaten by some vampires in Owosso, then you seem to have survived my daughter's pain-cakes and finally that police officer saves you from the feared and loathsome labor organizers of Detroit! You are truly blessed."

Lefty Lewis was back to acting normal, but I kept wondering what was in the box he didn't want the cop to see.

I said, "What's a labor organizer, sir?"

Mr. Lewis said, "In Flint they are people who are trying to get unions in the automobile factories."

Before I had a chance to get my next question in Lefty Lewis said, "I'ma save your breath for you, Bud. I'll bet the next thing out of your mouth was going to be, 'What's a union,' right?"

"Yes, sir."

"A union is like a family, it's when a group of workers get together and try to make things better for themselves and their children."

"That's all, sir?"

"That's all."

"Then why are the cops after them?"

"That's a very good question. Look in that box you put under your seat."

I pulled the box out and put it in my lap and looked over at Lefty Lewis. He looked back at me and checked the rearview mirror. "Go ahead."

I stopped for a second. Maybe there was a loaded and cocked pistol hiding in the box, maybe Lefty Lewis *would've* shot it out with the cop if he'd tried to take us to jail.

I started raising the top off the box, and just as I was about to get it open Lefty Lewis moved a lot faster than you'd think somebody's granddad could and slapped his hand on top of it closing it back tight.

Uh-oh. Maybe this was loot from a bank that him and Al Capone had knocked over! Maybe Lefty Lewis would have to rub me out if I saw what was inside! Maybe if I looked I'd know too much!

He said, "Before you look, Bud, you've got to understand that what's in there is very dangerous."

I said, "Well, sir, I really don't think I need to see it, sir. I think I'll just look out the window until we get to Grand Rapids, or maybe . . ." I gave a big fake yawn. "Maybe I'll take a nap."

He laughed and said, "Ah, you're a lot smarter than you look, Bud, you know it would've been curtains for us if that copper would've seen what's in there." He tapped the top of the box.

All I could say was, "Yes, sir."

He said, "Go ahead and open it. But! You have to promise—no, you have to swear that you won't breathe a word about what you see to anyone."

"Mr. Lewis, sir, I'd really rather take a nap."

"Well, first open the box."

I took in a big gulp of air and started to raise the top off the box again.

Lefty Lewis yelled, "Bud!"

I jumped so high I nearly banged my head on the roof of the car.

I yelled back, "Yes, sir?"

"I didn't hear you swear to keep your lips locked."

"Aw, shucks, Mr. Lewis, I swear, but I'd feel a lot better if I could take a doggone nap."

I snatched the top off the box and got ready to be scared to death.

It was just some paper with writing on it.

Maybe the pistol or the loot was under all this paper. I kept lifting paper until I got to the bottom of the box. Nothing!

I looked at Lefty Lewis. He said, "I warned you, pretty dangerous, isn't it?"

I must've missed something. I went through the box again.

"How's some paper dangerous, sir?"

"Read it."

I took one of the papers out, it said:

ATTENTION RAILROAD WORKERS

THE NEWLY FORMED GRAND RAPIDS
BRANCH OF THE BROTHERHOOD OF
PULLMAN PORTERS WILL BE HOLDING AN
INFORMATIONAL MEETING ON WEDNESDAY,
JULY 23, 1936. ALL INTERESTED PARTIES
PLEASE COME TO 2345 COLDBROOK AT 9:00.

REFRESHMENTS WILL BE SERVED.
YOU KNOW WHAT WE'RE UP AGAINST—
PLEASE KEEP THIS AS CONFIDENTIAL AS POSSIBLE.

It was starting to make sense. I said, "Mr. Lewis, are you one of those labor organizers?"

He laughed. "Not really, Bud. I'm picking these up so we can pass them out in Grand Rapids. We've been negotiating to get a union for the Pullman porters for years now and nowhere in Grand Rapids will print these flyers for us. The only place that would do them is all the way in Flint. You were running away to a pretty hot town, young man."

"Wow!"

"That trouble the policeman was talking about at the factory is called a sit-down strike. Instead of walking in front of the plant with signs the people who are on strike just sit down on their job. That way the bosses can't bring other people in to steal their jobs. They're going to sit there until the company gives them a union, so the company is trying everything they can think of to get them out. That's why I said those flyers are so dangerous. The people who run the factories and the railroads seemed to be really scared. To them if a worker has any dignity or pride he can't be doing a good job."

BOY, THESE AUTOMOBILES were great for making you conk out! Between the car floating real soft down the

139

road and Lefty Lewis's boring stories about the railroad and the union and baseball I was out cold in no time.

When I woke up I looked out the window and stretched.

Lefty Lewis said, "I was about to take you to Butterworth Hospital, I thought you'd left the earth for good."

He pointed out of the window and said, "Looking familiar?"

Uh-oh. "Yes, sir." I pointed at a gasoline filling station and said, "Yup, there's the gasoline filling station."

He said, "I guess your daddy would have to burn premium in that big Packard, wouldn't he? I don't think those big engines can run on ethyl gasoline."

I said, "No, sir, that's right."

He told me, "Well, you and your daddy sure have one beautiful machine."

I was getting real nervous but I said, "Thank you, sir."

We turned another corner and my heart started jumping around in my stomach. Halfway down the street was a building that looked like it was made out of giant chopped-down trees. The Log Cabin!

Uh-oh. Right outside the place was a sign that said, AP-PEARING FRIDAY THROUGH SUNDAY IN JULY HERMAN E. CALLOWAY AND THE NUBIAN KNIGHTS OF THE NEW DEAL.

My father had joined a new band!

Lefty Lewis pulled up next to a car that was as long as a big boat.

He said, "Ah, there's the Packard, he's here."

I had to think real fast. I couldn't let Mr. Lewis and Herman E. Calloway talk to each other. If they did I'd be on the first thing smoking back to Flint. And besides, I felt kind of bad about lying to Mr. Lewis, I wished I didn't have to.

Lefty Lewis cut the car off and pulled the key out of the dashboard.

I said, "Mr. Lewis, this is going to be very embarrassing for me."

"What is, Bud?"

"Can I go talk to my father by myself, sir? I swear I'll turn myself in to him."

Lefty Lewis looked at me kind of hard. "Well, Bud, I don't mean to sully your reputation, but you just ran away from that man all the way across the state, I think I'd better hand-deliver you."

"But Mr. Lewis, sir, I need to explain it to him by myself. I promise I'll go in and not run away again."

Lefty Lewis looked out of the windshield like he was thinking. He reached back across the seat and put his hand on the twine keeping my suitcase together. He said, "I'll tell you what, Bud, you don't go anywhere without this, do you?"

I said, "No, sir."

"OK, here's the deal, I'll give you"—he looked at his wristwatch—"five minutes to talk to your dad alone. If you're not back by then I'll bring your bag in for you."

It wasn't great, but it would have to do. Besides, it gave me some more time to think.

"Please promise that you won't look inside of it, sir."

He raised his hand. "You've got my word."

I got out of the car and walked to the front of the Log Cabin. The doors looked like they were made out of chopped-down trees just like the rest of the building. I looked back at Lefty Lewis and he was still watching so I opened one of the doors.

I knew it was one of those doors that Momma had been talking about. I walked in to see what was going to happen.

Shucks, there was another set of regular doors inside. The front door closed behind me and I was in the dark. I tried the other door and it came open but I didn't push it all the way in.

I waited, then went back out to get my bag.

I walked over to the driver's side of Lefty Lewis's car, smiled and said, "Thank you very much, sir. He's in there, he was so glad to see me that I'm not even in a whole lot of trouble. He's real busy right now and told me to tell you thank you very much and that he'd get a holt of you."

Lefty Lewis smiled too. "Well, he might be happy now, but if I know anything about your daddy I expect you're gonna be having problems sitting down before this night's over.

"Now I know he's going to tell you this but I gotta add my two cents. Son, there just aren't too many places a young Negro boy should be traveling by himself, especially not clear across Michigan, there're folks in this state that make your average Ku Kluxer look like John Brown. You know who John Brown is?"

"Uh-uh, no, sir."

"That's all right, he's out there moldering somewhere. But the point is you were very lucky this time. You've got to be good and stay put. I know your dad's not the easiest man in the world but, believe me, he's mellowed a lot from when it was just him and your sister.

"The next time you're of a mind to do a little traveling you come on down to the train station and ask for Lefty Lewis first. I won't tell anyone, but we need to talk before you set out on your own again. Lefty Lewis. Think you can remember that name?"

"Lefty Lewis." Well, at least he was using the alias all over and not just with me and his family in Flint.

He handed my bag out of the window. "OK, get back on in there and tell your daddy I said hello."

"Thank you, Mr. Lewis."

I stood waving until the big car turned out into the street.

I sucked in a jumbo gulp of air and opened the front door again. This time I pushed the second set of doors open and walked in.

It was dark but I could see that there were six men sitting in a circle on a little stage at the other end of the room. One of them was white.

Five of the men had their eyes on the other guy. One of them had drumsticks in his hands and was leaned over softly tapping out a rhythm on the wooden stage floor. Three of them were drinking from bottles of pop, and one, a real old one, was using a rag to wipe the inside of a trumpet. The guy who had to be my father was sitting with his back to me wearing a hat.

He was talking just like me! And it didn't take much listening to tell he was lying, or at least doing some real good exaggerating, just like I do!

That was all the proof I needed.

His voice was a lot rougher and more tired-sounding than I thought it would be. He leaned back in his chair. "That's right, after I won the Golden Gloves no one couldn't tell me I wasn't going to be middleweight champ within two, three years tops."

The drummer stopped tapping. "Middleweight? What, this was so long ago gravity wasn't as strong as it is now, or did a pound just weigh less back then?"

The others laughed but my dad didn't let it bother him. "That's right, middleweight. You got to keep in mind that I had more hair and fewer pounds back then."

He pulled the hat off and rubbed his hands over his

glass-smooth head. My dad shaved his hair! That was something I always wanted to do too!

He said, "My manager goes and lines up a bout against a fighter outta Chicago by the name of Jordan 'Snaggletooth' MacNevin.

"From the name I'm expecting some young Irish kid with bad teeth but this guy was one of us and so old that he could have been a waiter at the Last Supper.

"When the fight began I wasn't about to show mercy, you understand?"

All the guys onstage were nodding.

"And to make a long story longer I go out and flick this halfway stiff right jab clean at Pops's head and—"

The horn guy said, "Herman, to this day I can't believe you swung at that old man."

"What was I supposed to do, Jimmy? I wasn't trying to kill him or nothing, I just wanted to put him down quick and quiet."

Jimmy went, "Uh, uh, uh . . ."

"And the next thing I know I'm watching my mouth-piece and my chance to be champ flying out of the ring into the fourth row of seats. I ain't never been hit so hard in my life."

The drummer said, "What, you lost one fight and quit?"

Then Herman E. Calloway said the words that let me know I was right. I felt like someone had cut a light on inside me. I knew it'd been right for me to come all the way from Flint to Grand Rapids to find my dad.

The idea that had started as a teeny-weeny seed in a suitcase was now a mighty maple.

Herman E. Calloway, my father, said, "There comes a time when you're doing something and you realize it just doesn't make any sense to keep on doing it, you ain't being a quitter, it's just that the good Lord has seen fit to give you the sense to know, you understand, enough is enough."

That was the exact same thought I'd had when I got whipped by Toddy boy! Only two folks with the same blood would think them just alike! I sucked in a big gulp of air, got a good grip on my suitcase and walked into the light of the stage.

The old horn guy, Jimmy, saw me first and said, "I thought I heard that door open. Did Miss Thomas send you, son?"

I just kept walking onto the stage. I had to see my father's face, I knew we'd look so much alike that the truth would hit him as hard as that Snaggletooth guy had. Even Lefty Lewis said he could tell me and Herman E. Calloway were kin.

He turned to see who Jimmy was talking to and my mighty maple started shaking in the wind.

My dad's face was old.

My dad's face was real old, just like this horn guy.

Maybe too old. But . . . there was just too much proof that this was my father!

He smiled at me. He had his arms crossed over a great big stomach with his head-wiping rag hanging out of his right hand.

The first thing my dad said to me was, "Well, well, well, little man, what brings you here? Miss Thomas?"

"I don't know any Miss Thomas, sir."

"So what're you doing here?" He put his hand over his eyes to shield them from the stage lights and looked out into the dark part of the bar. I noticed how wrinkly my dad's hand was. "Who brought you here? Your folks out there?"

"No, sir. I'm here to meet my father."

Jimmy said, "Who's your daddy? Why'd he tell you to meet him here?"

I kept looking at Herman E. Calloway.

"He didn't tell me to meet him here, sir. I come all the way from Flint to meet my daddy for the very first time."

All the men looked over at the drummer. He stopped tapping.

He said, "Awww, man. Look, this child ain't no kin of mine. What's your momma's name, boy?"

I said, "You ain't my daddy." I pointed right at Herman E. Calloway's big belly. "You know it's you."

All the eyes jumped over on Herman E. Calloway. He

quit smiling and looked at me a lot harder, like he was really noticing me.

I knew if I was a regular kid I'd be crying buckets of tears now, I didn't want these men to think I was a baby so I was real glad that my eyes don't cry no more. My nose plugged up and a little growl came out of my mouth but I kept my finger pointed, cleared my throat and said, "I know it's you."

# CHAPTER 13

*THE CIRCLE OF MEN* got very quiet. The younger guys looked like they wanted to laugh but were afraid to and the Jimmy guy and the man who must be my father were looking at me that way grown-ups do when they're getting ready to give you some bad news or when they're trying to decide which hand they're going to smack you upside the head with.

Finally Jimmy snapped his fingers and said, "Hold on now, is your name Bud?"

He knew my name! I said, "Yes, sir!"

Jimmy said, "Herman, don't you see? This has something to do with that crazy telegram you got this morning." He looked back at me, "And you said you're from Flint, Bud?"

"Yes, sir, that's right, that's right where I'm from!"

Herman E. Calloway said, "What in Sam Hill is going on here? First off, don't you be coming in here accusing folks of being your father, and second off, where is your mother?"

Shucks, he said it like he didn't already know. I said, "She's dead, sir, she died four years ago."

Herman E. Calloway said, "I am truly sorry to hear that, but it's obvious that you are a disturbed young man and you don't have a clue who your father is. You just tell us who's looking after you now, and we'll get you sent back to wherever it is you belong."

"I belong with you now, sir."

Herman E. Calloway said, "Now you look here . . ."

Jimmy said, "Hold on, Herman." He seemed a lot nicer than this Calloway guy. "Bud, you got to understand Mr. Calloway here can't be your daddy, nohow, no way, nuh-uh. I don't know what gave you that idea, but whatever, we've got to get you back home. Someone in Flint's got to be worried sick about you."

I said, "No, sir, I don't have nobody left in Flint, that's why I came all the way here."

He said, "No one, no one at all?"

I said, "No, sir."

He said, "No brothers?"

"No, sir."

"No sisters?"

"No, sir."

"What about an auntie?"

"No, sir."

"No grandma?"

"No, sir."

Shucks, it looked like this guy was going to go over my whole family tree, but he whistled and said, "So were you living in an orphanage?"

Uh-oh, I had to be careful how I answered this, one wrong answer and I could tell that these guys were ready to give me up to the cops or give me a one-way ticket back to the Home.

I said, "Well, sir, I had some problems with some folks that were supposed to be looking after me and after I hid their shotgun and poured water all over Todd Amos I busted out of the shed and had to go on the lam and then I thought it was about time I came and met my father because it's been—"

He raised his hand to stop me.

"That's fine, son, but just answer what I asked you. What orphanage were you in?"

"Well, sir, I used to be in a Home and then I wasn't and then I was with some people that were kind of mean and then I tried to find Miss Hill but she moved all the way to Chicago and that was too far to walk so—"

He raised his hand again to shut me up.

"Hold on, Bud. Do me a favor, go wait by that door for a minute." He pointed to the side of the stage.

I walked over and waited to see what was going to happen. I tried pushing the door open a little bit in case I had to make a quick escape but it was jammed tight. I'd have to leave out of the same door I came in.

The man named Jimmy and the guy who had to be my daddy started whispering. After while Herman E. Calloway raised his arms and said, "Hey. But don't forget, this is your little red wagon, you pull it if you want."

Jimmy said, "Fair enough." He waved me back onto the stage.

"Bud," he said, "you look like you might be a little hungry, so I'll tell you what we're going to do. We're all done rehearsing and were about to head over to the Sweet Pea. You're invited to come along under one condition."

"What, sir?"

"Once you get something in your belly you've got to be straight with me, you've got some explaining to do, we'll feed you but you've got to tell us the truth. Do we have a deal?"

He stuck his hand out for me to shake. But I wanted to know what I was getting myself into.

"What's the Sweet Pea, sir?"

"Best restaurant in Grand Rapids. Is it a deal?"

I don't know how grown-ups can tell I'm always so

doggone hungry but I sure wasn't going to turn down getting my very first real restaurant food. I grabbed his hand and made sure I gave it a hard squeeze like Momma told me to and said, "Yes, sir. Thank you, sir."

He smiled. "No problem."

Herman E. Calloway said, "Well, James, like I said, if he's gonna be doing some explaining it's got to be to you, I don't need to listen to this scamp's nonsense whilst I'm trying to digest my supper."

He stuck a pipe that wasn't lit into his mouth and walked off the stage.

Shucks, if my father had to be so doggone old I was starting to wish that Lefty Lewis or this Jimmy guy were him, Herman E. Calloway seemed like he was going to be hard to get along with.

The horn player said, "Little man, my name is Jimmy Wesley, you can call me Mr. Jimmy."

"Yes, sir."

He pointed at the younger men. "The drummer there is Doug 'the Thug' Tennant, the sax man is Harrison Eddie 'Steady' Patrick . . ."

The saxophone player said, "Awww, man, it's not Eddie Steady, it's Steady Eddie, Steady Eddie Patrick."

Mr. Jimmy said, "Uh-huh, and on trombone we have Chug 'Doo-Doo Bug' Cross, and the palest member of the band, on piano, is Roy 'Dirty Deed' Breed."

He shook his head again and said, "Lord knows why these young musicians can't just leave the perfectly good names their mommas gave them alone, but for some reason they can't. Anyway, fellas, this here is Bud . . . what was your last name, Bud?"

"Caldwell, sir."

"This here's Bud Caldwell. He's gonna be our guest over at the Sweet Pea for dinner. Y'all say hello to the little man and make him feel comfortable."

The Thug said, "What's the word, Bud?"

Dirty Deed said, "How you doing?"

Doo-Doo Bug said, "Welcome, little stuff."

Steady Eddie said, "Good to meet you, my man."

I said, "Pleased to meet you."

Mr. Jimmy told them, "All right. He'll ride over with you four, me and Herm will meet you there."

The sax man, Steady Eddie, said, "All right, Mr. Jimmy, we'll finish loading up." The Jimmy guy went out the front door.

The sax man told me, "Come on, little man, if Mr. Jimmy's gonna spring for your supper the least you can do is help load the car. Grab that case over there and put it in the trunk of the Buick out back."

He pointed to a long skinny black suitcase that had a leather handle on top of it and said, "And be careful, that's my bread and butter in there."

I must have looked confused because he told me, "That's my horn, my ax, my saxophone, the thing I make all my money with, so don't get butterfingers and drop it."

154

I said, "Oh. Yes, sir."

The trombone man, Doo-Doo Bug, said, "One thing you are going to have to drop, though, is all that 'sir' stuff. The only two folks around here old enough for you to be calling them sir are Mr. Jimmy and"—he winked—"your long-lost dear old daddy."

The whole band busted a gut laughing.

The Thug guy said, "I'ma let you in on a little secret, my man. I think the only reason Mr. C. is denying he's your daddy is 'cause you went and hurt his feelings."

"How? I didn't do nothing to him."

"There it is, that's just what I mean. Here you two are getting together for the first time and you didn't show the man no love." He looked over at Doo-Doo Bug. "Bug, did you see any love being passed from this boy to his daddy?"

Doo-Doo Bug said, "You leave me out of your nonsense."

The Thug kept going. "Shoot, man, seems to me like you should give the man his props, seems to me like you should've given the man a whole lot more affection.

"You see, I know Mr. C. better than most folks do, I know that beneath that coldhearted, evil, wicked, nasty, mean—"

Doo-Doo Bug said, "Don't forget cheap, cheap's got to be in there somewhere."

The Thug said, "You know cheap's right up high on the list. But as I was saying, beneath all that festering nastiness is a tender, kind, loving human being. Why, I'd bet you dollars to doughnuts that he's outside right now sitting in that Packard sobbing openly about how you shunned him.

"When you get to the Sweet Pea, rush right up on him, give him a big hug, yell out 'Daddy,' then plant a big juicy kiss right on the top of his shiny bald head. Shoot, you do that and you'll be in his will so quick your head will spin."

I put this Thug guy on my list of people not to pay any mind to. Herman E. Calloway seemed like the kind of person that would rather get bit in the behind by a snaggletooth mule than have somebody give him a kiss.

Steady Eddie said, "Let's not get the little man killed before he's had a chance to eat, Thug. Son, I hope you've got sense enough to let what he's telling you to go in one ear and find the nearest exit. You just steer clear of Mr. C. for a while, he's not someone you want to toy with, and for God's sake whatever you do don't call him Daddy or Poppa or anything that's going to give anyone the idea you two are kin, you hear?"

These guys really thought I was dumb. I said, "Yes, sir. But isn't it just like my luck to come clean across the state to find my daddy and he turns out to be a mean old coot?"

I slapped my hand over my mouth, I knew better than saying something like this out loud but it just fell out of my mouth before I could swallow it down. This was Bud Caldwell's Rules and Things to Have a Funner Life and Make a Better Liar Out of Yourself Number 63.

### RULES AND THINGS NUMBER 63

**Never, Ever Say Something Bad About Someone You Don't Know—Especially When You're Around a Bunch of Strangers. You Never Can Tell Who Might Be Kin to That Person or Who Might Be a Lip-Flapping, Big-Mouth Spy.**

Sure enough, the drummer, the Thug guy, started acting like he was writing stuff down on a piece of pretend paper. He said, "Let's see, was that 'mean old coot' or 'old mean coot'? Shoot, baby, if I drop some info like this on Mr. C. I might be able to stay in this band longer than the last three drummers did. You see, kid, you ain't the only one trying to get on Mr. C.'s good side, this is the best drumming gig in the state and I need to hang on to it as long as I can."

I wasn't sure if this drummer guy really was a dirty dog or if he was just a big teaser. Whichever way, I'd have to work real hard on remembering Rule and Thing Number 68. Or was it 63?

Steady Eddie said, "Thug, you're gonna have to lay off the kid's chops, the little man's got problems enough and he sure don't need to have you meddling with him.

Let's get that car loaded, me and . . . what's your name again, kid?"

"Bud, not Buddy, si . . . just Bud, not Buddy."

"Right, me and Bud-not-Buddy are too dang hungry to hear any more of your lip."

Of all the Dusky Devastators of the Depression or the Nubian Knights, Steady Eddie is my favorite.

We loaded a bunch of funny-shaped black suitcases into the trunk of a big old black Buick, then climbed in. I got in the backseat and sat between Dirty Deed and Steady Eddie with my suitcase on my lap. Doo-Doo Bug got behind the steering wheel and the Thug got in beside him.

The Thug said, "So, Bud-not-Buddy, I'ma come right out and ask what's on everyone else's mind. How'd you find out Mr. C. was your daddy?"

"My mother let me know."

Thug said, "Uh, I ain't trying to be funny, and I'd never play the dozens on no one, but let me ask you, was your momma, uh, how can I put this? Was your momma as old as sand when she had you?"

Steady Eddie said, "Man, leave the kid alone, you got no call to go prying into his life."

I never minded talking about my momma so I told the Thug, "Yes, sir, she was pretty old when I was born."

Thug said, "Shoot, I knew she had to be either old or

crazy to have anything to do with that man. How old was she, eighty, and was she blind?"

I said, "No, sir, she was old, but her eyes didn't go bad yet. She was twenty when I was born, and she was twenty-six when she died."

That news always kills any conversation you're having with grown folks. The Dusky Devastators got as quiet as some mice with bedroom slippers on. The only sound you could hear for a second was the keys *cling-clang-cling*ing up against the metal dashboard as Doo-Doo Bug turned the car into the front of a little house that had a sign saying THE SWEET PEA on it.

The Thug said, "Things is hard all over, ain't they?"

Steady Eddie said, "You're all right, little man, you're a tough little nut, I like that. Most folks your age would be bawling their eyes out if they got teased as hard as that fool drummer was teasing you, but you ain't even close to crying, are you?"

I said, "No, sir, I don't know why, but my eyes don't cry no more."

Steady Eddie said, "I like that, 'my eyes don't cry no more.' You mind if I borrow that? That sounds like a great name for a song."

I said, "No, sir, I don't mind at all."

He reached over and rubbed his hand over my head and said, "Yeah, you're all right, little fella. And don't you worry none too much about the Thug, Mr. C.

changes drummers the way most folks change their drawers. What you see in that front seat is a man on borrowed time."

Thug said, "Awww, man, what did you hear?"

Doo-Doo Bug cut the car off and said, "All right, gentlemen, that's enough, let's go stuff our craws."

# CHAPTER 14

WHEN WE GOT into the restaurant I could
see that it was someone's living room that they'd set
about ten card tables and some folding chairs in. Every
table but one was filled and there were five or six people
standing in the doorway waiting to sit down. We said,
"Excuse us," and walked right past. Then the smell of
the place got into my nose and I could tell why folks
were lining up to get in.

I closed my eyes and took in a big snort of air. It was
like someone took a old pot and poured about a hundred

gallons of hot apple cider and a hundred gallons of hot coffee into it, then stirred eight or nine sweet potato pies, crusts and all, into that, then let six big steamy meat loafs float on top of all that, then threw in a couple of handfuls of smashed potatoes, then boiled the whole thing on high. This must be exactly how heaven smells!

I could tell by the smell that Mr. Jimmy was telling the truth when he said this was the best restaurant in Grand Rapids. Shucks, I've never eaten in one before but I'd say this was the best restaurant in the world! I opened my eyes 'cause the smell was starting to get me dizzy.

On the other side of the room Herman E. Calloway was sitting at a table with Mr. Jimmy and a woman.

Steady Eddie pointed at the only empty table, one that had a sign saying RESERVED NBC on top of it, and said, "That's where we're at, over there, Bud. NBC stands for 'Nobody but Calloway,' Mr. C. changes the name of the band so much that no one can keep up with the new names so they call us NBC so's they don't have to change the sign."

Before I could sit down with them Mr. Jimmy saw us and said, "Here they are," and pointed at me and waved for me to come over to their table. Shucks, I'd rather sit with the band than with Herman E. Calloway, it would be hard to have a good time eating if you looked up and saw him every time you took a bite.

The Thug said, "Remember what I said," pointed at

the top of his head and acted like he was smacking some kisses.

I walked to the other table.

Mr. Jimmy said, "Bud, this here's Miss Thomas, she's our vocal stylist."

She could tell I didn't know what that meant so she said, "I'm the singer, honey."

I said, "Pleased to meet you, ma'am."

She laughed and stuck her hand out for me to shake. There were about nine diamond rings on just her right hand!

She said, "Oh, my, a gentleman. I'm pleased to make your acquaintance as well."

Then she took all those ringed-up fingers and rubbed them across my cheek, held my chin and said, "Come here, child," and pulled my face up close to hers.

Uh-oh, I twisted up my face to get ready for a kiss but instead she looked real close at me and said, "What's this, baby?" She rubbed her fingers over a couple of sting spots that I'd been scratching.

For a second I was going to tell her they were vampire bites, but something told me to tell the truth this time. I said, "That's just some hornet stings, ma'am, I got bit up when the Amoses locked me in their shed."

It was her turn to twist her face up. "When *who* locked you up in *what* shed?"

"They were the people the Home was paying to look after me. I got bit by their fish-head guards." I showed the woman the bite on my hand. I was surprised to see it was puffing out from pus.

"My Lord!" she said. "Herman, this child's hand is infected. None of you men noticed how he looks?"

Herman E. Calloway said, "Talk to James, far as I know he's the only one who looked at the kid."

Mr. Jimmy said, "Well, Grace, to be truthful I did think the boy's face was a little swole up, but you know how dark it is in the Cabin, and, by God, there are some folks who just naturally have lopsided heads."

She said, "Dark or not, even Blind Lemon Jefferson could see something's wrong with this baby's eye. What happened here, Bud?" She touched underneath my eye as light as a feather.

I said, "Well, ma'am, Todd Amos woke me up by shoving a pencil up my nose all the way to the *R* and when I went to punch him I slapped him instead and it left a big welt on his cheek so we put up our dukes and went at it and it didn't take long before I knew I couldn't whip him so I just curled up and fell down."

I looked at Herman E. Calloway to make sure he was listening to the next part. I wanted to let him know that even though he was real mean our minds thought about things in the exact same way.

I said, "I fell down, ma'am, 'cause the Lord give me the good sense to know when enough is enough."

He acted like he didn't hear. So I kept talking to Miss

Thomas. "Then Mrs. Amos came and I could tell they'd gone through my suitcase even though they promised they wouldn't and she locked me up in the shed where those hornets and fish-head guards got a holt of me."

Miss Thomas looked like this was some real amazing news.

Herman E. Calloway said, "Sounds like a case of diarrhea of the mouth and constipation of the brain."

Miss Thomas gave him a dirty look and said, "You said 'the Home,' Bud, what kind of a home? Where's your momma?"

I said, "She died four years ago, ma'am."

She put her hand on my shoulder and said, "I'm sorry, sweetheart. How 'bout your daddy? Do you know where he's at?"

I said, "Yes, ma'am."

She said, "Where is he, honey?"

I pointed dead at Herman E. Calloway's big belly again and said, "That's him right there."

Miss Thomas looked like she wanted to smile but she said, "Now, Bud, I've only known you for a couple of minutes but I can tell your momma did a fine job of raising you, I can see you've had a good, proper upbringing, so I'm kind of surprised that you're pointing like that."

She was right. I brought my finger down. I said, "I'm sorry, ma'am."

She said, "That's fine, but it wasn't me who got pointed at."

I told Herman E. Calloway, "I'm sorry, sir." But I didn't mean it.

She smiled and said, "That's better, we all make mistakes. You know what, Bud, you look like you could use a good meal, so why don't you sit right there and join us?" She pointed a ring-covered finger at the empty chair direct across from him.

Shucks, how could anyone enjoy their food with Herman E. Calloway staring back at you?

But maybe my luck was starting to change. As soon as I sat down, Herman E. Calloway picked up his coffee cup and said, "If you'll excuse me, this is about where I came in," and walked over to where the band was sitting.

He told them, "All right. Someone's got to give me their seat and go sit with James and Miss Grace—oh, and my son."

For a second it looked like a stampede of Dusky Devastators of the Depression, they all jumped up at once and started heading for our table.

They saw what they'd done, laughed, and Steady Eddie said, "Take my seat, Mr. C., I wanna talk to that kid, he's got the look of a future sax man about him."

He came over to our table.

Miss Thomas asked me, "Do you mind if I order your supper, Bud?"

I said, "No, ma'am." I couldn't believe you got to order what you wanted, I thought you just sat down and they'd bring you whatever was on the stove.

A woman came up to the table. She said, "Y'all ready, Miss Thomas?"

Miss Thomas said, "We sure are, Tyla."

Tyla said, "Who's the little fella, did y'all pick up someone new for the band?"

Miss Thomas laughed. "They're getting younger all the time, aren't they? This here's Bud and he's going to be our guest for a while, so I want to impress him with something special."

Tyla said, "Well, you know you brought him to the right place. It's nice to meet you, Bud."

I said, "Pleased to meet you, ma'am."

She said, "Ma'am? Mercy, Miss Thomas, your guest has some real fine manners. I can tell that he isn't one of those rude, crude folks Mr. Calloway usually scours up."

Steady Eddie said, "Tyla, I am crushed."

She said, "Bud, I apologize for mistaking you for a musician."

I told her, "That's OK, ma'am, no offense taken."

Miss Thomas said, "Is there any more of that meat loaf left?"

"Yes, ma'am, sure is."

"How about some okra and mashed potatoes too, Bud?"

"Thank you, ma'am."

"And does a glass of apple cider sound good?"

"Yes, ma'am, thank you, ma'am."

"OK," she said, "I'll have the same."

Mr. Jimmy ordered a supper that was all the way different from mine and Steady Eddie ordered one that was all the way different from his! No wonder you hear about rich folks going to restaurants once a week, this was great!

Miss Tyla went away and Miss Thomas started back on me.

"Bud, I've got to let you know that I'm pretty sure that there's just no way that Mr. C. is your father. Tell me what gave you the idea he was."

"My mother did, ma'am."

Miss Thomas looked over at Mr. Jimmy real quick, then said, "Sweetheart, did you know a whole lot of people all over the state know Mr. C., did you know he's pretty famous?"

"No, ma'am."

"Ah, well. You know what I think? I think maybe your mother heard him on the radio or heard somebody talking about him or saw the band somewhere and told you that Mr. C. reminded her of your father and you misunderstood what she meant, isn't that possible?"

"I don't think so, ma'am."

She looked at me for a second, then said, "Did she come right out and say, 'Your daddy is Herman E. Calloway,' Bud?"

"Well, almost. But not in words just like that."

"Then tell me what the words were like, honey."

Uh-oh. It was going to be hard to explain to Miss Thomas about mighty maples and hints from flyers. As long as I kept Herman E. Calloway being my father to myself the whole thing made real good sense, but as soon as I tried to tell other folks about it, it seemed like maybe it was something some stupid kid had dreamed up, like it was wishing and hoping instead of something true and real.

I looked down at my suitcase and said, "Well . . ."

And I could tell my luck *was* changing, before I could say anything else Miss Tyla was at our table with a tray.

Miss Thomas reached across the table, patted my hand and said, "We'll talk tomorrow, Bud, I bet you're sick and tired of answering people's questions, aren't you?"

I said, "Yes, ma'am, I am." But I did notice that she'd said "tomorrow." That might mean they weren't going to try to send me back to Flint right away!

Miss Tyla said, "Miss Thomas," and set a plate in front of her, then said, "Mr. Jimmy," and gave him some food too, then said, "Steady," and put his plate down so that it rattled a little, then said, "And finally, the young gentleman," and put a plate crammed with food in front of me!

It was the best meal I'd ever had, and when it was done Miss Tyla brought me a dessert she called "On the

House." It was a piece of warm sweet potato pie with some white fluffy stuff called whipped cream swopped all over the top of it.

After I shoved the last crumbs of pie in my mouth and scraped up the last little dribbles of whipped cream, I looked around at the people at my table and I couldn't help breaking out in a big smile.

I didn't see it before, but now that I looked I could tell that Miss Thomas must be the most beautiful woman in the world. When she talked she moved her hands and fingers around and the lights from the ceiling and from the little candle on the table would bounce off all them diamonds and spark up in your eye and make you feel like you'd been hit with some kind of magic fairy dust, then you couldn't help but smile.

All the while she'd hum too, but *hum* doesn't seem like it's the right word for what she was doing. Most times I'd heard humming before it was just a excuse for not being able to sing or something people'd do if they didn't know the words to a song. Uh-uh, that doesn't fit the sounds Miss Thomas was making, you couldn't help but look up and wonder if this was a real human bean that was making these sounds.

What her humming reminded me most of was that feeling you get when you walk barefoot on a railroad track and, for a long time before you can see it, you can feel the train coming right through the bottoms of your feet. Her humming started slow and easy at first, but then, just like you could feel that train shake-a-shake-a-shaking from somewhere far off, after while Miss Thomas's humming made you feel like something big and strong was passing right by you and everything on you was getting rattly and shaky and about to get shook loose. It made you want to drop your fork and grab holt of something solid.

From hearing just this little bit of humming I could understand why Mr. Jimmy didn't call her a singer, *singer* wasn't a big enough word to take in the kind of music that was jumping out of Miss Thomas's chest.

And I didn't notice before how funny Mr. Jimmy was. The stories he was telling about traveling around the country with Herman E. Calloway had us all laughing so much that even the nosy people at all the tables near ours quit eating and were busting their guts and throwing their two cents into the stories.

The only table that was quiet was where the Dusky Devastators were sitting. It seemed like Herman E. Calloway could make it so you just wanted to sit and watch your hands with a sad look on your face.

And I hadn't noticed before how nice Steady Eddie was either. He talked out of the side of his mouth and kept his eyes kind of blinked halfway down, especially when Miss Tyla would come to our table to see if we were all right, which she did a lot. And he was the first person I'd ever seen who could eat and talk and laugh and drink and sneeze whilst keeping a toothpick dangling out of his mouth, no matter what he'd do that toothpick always stayed dancing just below his mustache. And Steady Eddie took his time to show me how to hold my lips and how to put my fingers like I was really playing a pretend saxophone.

I'm not sure exactly when it happened, if it was when I was scraping up the last little drops of melted whipped cream or if it was when Miss Thomas's fingers got to flinging all that magic fairy dust, but sometime whilst I was sitting in the Sweet Pea another seed got to sprouting, sometime in that smells-like-heaven place another mighty maple started digging down its roots and grabbing holt.

One second I was laughing my head off and the next second I was feeling very surprised 'cause something hit me just as hard as Snaggletooth MacNevin had smacked Herman E. Calloway. All of a sudden I knew that of all the places in the world that I'd ever been in this was the one. That of all the people I'd ever met these were the ones. This was where I was supposed to be.

And Herman E. Calloway could kiss my wrist if he thought he was gonna scare me out of this. It was gonna take more than a grouchy old bald-headed guy with a tremendous belly to run me out of here.

I was smiling and laughing and busting my gut so much that I got carried away and some rusty old valve squeaked open in me then . . . woop, zoop, sloop . . . tears started jumping out of my eyes so hard that I had to cover my face with the big red and white napkin that was on the table.

I hadn't been this embarrassed since I woke up and found Mrs. Sleet looking at my legs. I could tell that everyone in the Sweet Pea had stopped laughing and talking and had started looking at me, but I still couldn't quit bawling. Momma used to tell me I'd only get one chance to make a first impression and it looked like I was blowing it with the Dusky Devastators of the Depression.

Shucks. Finally I had to put my face in my arms on top of the table and put the napkin over my head like it was a little blanket 'cause, try as hard as I wanted, it didn't look like I was gonna get this doggone valve closed any time soon.

I felt Miss Thomas's hand come up under the napkin and rub real soft and slow back and forth over my head. She pulled me out of my chair into her lap and wrapped her arms around me and bounced me up and down on her knee. Dangee, I'd never have any kind of reputation with the band now, the only thing I could do was hang on to the napkin and try to make it so folks wouldn't notice how wet my face was.

She said, so quiet that I was the only one who could hear it, "OK, baby, OK. I know, sweetheart, I know." Then she started humming again and with my ear mashed up against her chest it felt like all my bones and muscles quit doing their jobs, it felt like something as big as a steam locomotive engine was chug-chug-chugging right past my ear.

I wasn't sure if it was her lips or her hand, but something whispered to me in a language that I didn't have any trouble understanding, it said, "Go ahead and cry, Bud, you're home."

# CHAPTER 15

*"Now, Bud,"* Miss Thomas said, "this is what we call Grand Calloway Station." She parked the car in front of a big house and got out so I grabbed my suitcase from the backseat and jumped out too.

Even though I was still real embarrassed and quiet about all the crying I'd just been doing at the Sweet Pea I knew I was going to have to start talking sooner or later so I asked her, "How come this house has got a name, ma'am?"

She said, "Mr. Calloway said a long time ago that

there were so many different people in and out of here at so many different hours of the day and night that it reminded him of that train station in New York City, Grand Central Station. The name kind of stuck."

As soon as we got inside Miss Thomas said, "I'll show you around the place tomorrow, tonight it's late and we're all pretty tired, so I'll take you right up to where you're going to be sleeping."

I followed her up a staircase and we walked down a hall. Miss Thomas opened a door and we went in. On one side there was a bed and a window with some curtains, and on the other side were two little doors. Sitting in the space between the two doors was a chair and a little table like the kind you see in the moving pictures that women use to put lipstick on, it had a long skinny drawer that went across the bottom and a big round mirror stuck right on top. Next to the bed there was a little table with a lamp that had a picture of a skinny little black horse right in the lampshade.

Miss Thomas turned on the lamp and the horse got all bright, now I could see he was brown. Miss Thomas said, "We're going to have to talk to Mr. Calloway about where you can put your things, Bud, I don't think you'll be able to fit anything in those closets." She pointed at the two little doors. "There're a lot of old things in there that he really needs to clear out. For now just put your suitcase there." She pointed at the table with the mirror on it.

I said, "Yes, ma'am, thank you, ma'am."

She smiled and said, "OK, I guess that's it. The first door in the hall on the left is my room, the second door is Mr. Calloway's, and the door on the right is the bathroom. Do you think you'll be all right?"

I would, except that those two little doors were starting to make me nervous. They looked like they were just the right size for a young Frankenstein or wolfman to come busting out of once all the grown folks left the room, and since there was only one chair in the room I wouldn't be able to block both of the doors off.

I said, "I'll probably be OK, ma'am, but there's one thing I'm wondering about."

"What's that, sweetheart?"

I pointed at the doors and said, "Are those locked?"

I was going to have to try to make a better first impression on Miss Thomas, she had to think I was pretty babyish what with me crying my eyes out before and now being scared of some little monster-size doors.

She laughed and said, "I don't think they're locked, Bud, there's nothing in there but girl's clothes and toys."

I said, "Won't the girl get mad if she comes back in here and I'm sleeping in her bed?"

Miss Thomas waited a second like she had to think. She finally said, "No, Bud, I don't think you have to worry about that, she's gone."

Uh-oh! That was two things to get nervous about in

one sentence! The first thing to worry about was Rules and Things number 547, or something, that was the one about when a adult tells you, "Don't worry." The second bad thing was Bud Caldwell's Rules and Things to Have a Funner Life and Make a Better Liar Out of Yourself Number 28, that was a real short one:

### RULES AND THINGS NUMBER 28

**Gone = dead!**

I don't know why grown folks can't say someone is dead, they think it's a lot easier to say "gone."

That meant I was going to have to spend the night in the room of a little dead girl, that meant I wasn't going to be getting much sleep at all. I could jam the chair up against the one door's knob, and I'd have to scooch the table with the mirror over up against the other one. I don't buy it when people tell you that closets are the only way a ghost or monster can get into your room. Shucks, I bet you they got ways to come up from under your bed, or if they want to get at you real bad, I bet they can even slide out of a drawer that you think is shut good and tight.

Miss Thomas said, "I'll see you in the morning, you get a good night's sleep." She closed the door and was gone just like that.

Before you could say Jack Robinson I had the chair jammed up underneath the one doorknob and was trying to figure out the best way to push the dresser thing when I heard some loud voices coming from out in the hall. It was Herman E. Calloway and Miss Thomas going at each other pretty good.

They argued back and forth so I sat on the bed and put my suitcase in my lap hoping that Mr. Calloway would win the argument and they'd give me some other place to sleep. I can never get why grown folks will put a kid all alone in a bedroom at night. It's just like they give the ghosts a treasure map and instead of there being a big pot of gold where X marks the spot, there's some poor kid that's sound asleep.

The door banged open and Herman E. Calloway stood there huffing and puffing like the big bad wolf, only with his belly it looked like he'd already eaten the three little pigs. I wasn't too worried because I could see the toes of Miss Thomas's shoes in the doorway.

Herman E. Calloway looked at me sitting on the bed and rushed over to the first little closet door. With one mighty huff he swiped the ghost-blocking chair away and stuck a key in the lock. Then he stomped over to the other closet door and locked it too.

He kind of whispered so Miss Thomas couldn't hear. "You've got the rest of them fooled, but not me. There's something about you that I don't like. I'm going to find out what your game is and believe you me, scamp, you're going back where you belong."

He stuck the key back in his pants pocket, walked out of the room and slammed the door.

The door wasn't even done shaking from being slammed so hard when it jumped open again. Herman E. Calloway pointed a finger at me and said, "And you better not do any snooping around this room or anywhere else in this house, I know where every single thing belongs and I can tell right away when something's missing. I've got little secret bells all over everything and when something's stolen the bell goes off and only I can hear it, so watch your step."

The poor door got slammed again.

Miss Thomas said, "You know, Herman, half the time I don't know if I should laugh at you or just feel sorry for you."

What Herman E. Calloway said reminded me of what they used to tell us when they'd take us kids from the Home to the YMCA to go swimming.

Before we'd start swimming the white lifeguard made us sit on the edge of the pool with just our feet in the water. He'd say, "We've had problems with you children urinating in the pool in the past, we've begged you and pleaded with you to stop but you don't seem to get the message. This has forced the Y to spend a great deal of money to put a special new kind of magic chemical in the water.

"This chemical reacts to turn water contaminated with urine a bright red. Therefore, if you urinate in the pool a bright red cloud will surround you and we will be able to tell who has relieved themselves. The chemical also causes severe burns to the skin of the urinater.

"So if a red cloud appears around any of you people you will be arrested by the Flint police, you will go to the hospital to fix your burns, you will go to jail and then your name will go on the list that says you can't swim in any pool in any building anywhere in the world.

"If a red cloud appears around any of you people you will from that moment on be swimming nowhere but in the Flint River."

Shucks, nothing makes you want to pee in a pool more than someone who thinks you're stupid telling you not to do it, and nothing makes you want to steal something more than having somebody who doesn't even know you're honest telling you not to steal.

Herman E. Calloway didn't have to worry, I was a liar, not a thief. The only thing I'd ever stole was food out of someone's garbage can.

He was so doggone mean and hard to get along with it just didn't seem like it was true that he could be anyone's daddy. The way he was so worried about me stealing stuff from him before he even knew if I was honest or not made me wonder if someone who was so suspicious could ever be kin to me.

I looked around the little dead girl's room and could

see that even a hard-up thief wouldn't find nothing much worth stealing in here.

The best thing in the whole room was one wall that was covered with pictures of some horses cut out of a bunch of magazines and stuck on the wall with thumb-tacks. It looked like someone went through a lot of trouble to do it, each picture was held up with four thumbtacks and there were so many of them that they were like wallpaper from the floor to the ceiling.

There might've been something good in the closets, but even before Herman E. Calloway'd locked them shut I sure wasn't about to peek in them.

I set my suitcase on the dressing table and looked at the first drawer. Like I said, someone telling you not to do something will sure make you want to do it. I listened real careful to make sure Herman E. Calloway wasn't sneaking up on me, then I pulled the drawer open.

There were three boxes of thumbtacks, and one of those doggone Ticonderoga pencils. Looking at it made me smell rubber all over again.

I walked over to the bed and sat on the edge and flopped back into the mattress.

Man! It was the softest thing I'd ever felt in my life, I rubbed my arms up and down on the blanket and pulled the pillow out and put it underneath my head. The bed had two sheets on it, just like Toddy boy's!

It was strange, even though this was the bedroom of some little girl who'd kicked the bucket, I wasn't feeling scared or nervous at all. I took in a deep, deep breath and it felt like I was sleeping with my own blanket wrapped around my head. I took in a couple more deep breaths and I could hear Momma starting to read another story to me.

I wanted to climb under the covers to see what it felt like to sleep with two sheets, but before I could even move . . . woop, zoop, sloop . . . I was sleeping like a dead man. The last thing I remember hearing was, "Not me," said the horse.

"Not me," said the sheep.

"Not me," said the werewolf.

I knew I was going to have a great sleep 'cause even though a monster had gone and snucked hisself into the story, I didn't care, nothing could hurt me now.

# CHAPTER 16

*I HAD TO FIGHT* like a tiger to wake up the next morning. The first thing I saw was those horses thumbtacked all over the wall. I stretched and noticed my shirt was off. I kicked my legs and could tell I was under the covers with one sheet underneath me and one sheet on top of me and my pants were off too.

Boy, I must've really been tired last night. I couldn't even remember getting undressed and getting between the sheets. But that explained why I was sleeping so hard, I found out one of rich people's secrets: Sleeping with two sheets puts you out like a baby that's been rode around in a automobile.

I looked over and thought I was dreaming. My clothes were all folded up in a neat pile the same way Momma used to fold them when she'd go to work before I got up. I blinked my eyes a couple of times 'cause it looked like there was a note on my clothes. Momma would always leave me a note that said something like, "Dear Bud, Please be neater, see you tonight, I love you."

My eyes started getting all sting-y but I blinked them a bunch more times and the note disappeared. I kept blinking but the pile of clothes stayed right where it was.

Aw, shucks, Miss Thomas must've come in at night and undressed me and put me in bed. I bet she got a real good look at my legs.

I got up as quiet as I could and put my clothes back on. I could hear laughing and talking coming from downstairs.

Right when I got near the kitchen door I could hear Herman E. Calloway saying, ". . . so that's how that cookie's going to crumble."

Miss Thomas said, "You have no idea how bad those orphanages can be, it's no place to be raised. I can't believe you, you'll take care of any stray dog wandering through this neighborhood, but when it comes to a child all of a sudden you have no sympathy. You might not have been paying attention, but we agreed last night what we were going to do about that boy, and that's what we're sticking to."

Uh-oh. I was glad I didn't take anything out of my suitcase, 'cause it looked like I might be making a break for the street again.

Herman E. Calloway said, "Like I said, I'ma find out what the real story is in Flint, and then we'll see."

Miss Thomas said, "That's fine, I believe the child. You, above all people, should know that I've got a sense about when someone is lying.'"

Uh-oh, I'd have to remember that.

She kept talking. "Until we've heard otherwise from Flint, he's staying right here."

A fourth voice said, "Well, I'm glad to hear it, that means I didn't go digging around in the basement for nothing. I think he's going to really like this."

It was Steady Eddie and it sounded like he had something for me!

I ran back up the steps on my tiptoes and down the hall to the little dead girl's room. I stood outside the room and closed the door loud enough that they could hear it downstairs. I *clump-clump-clump*ed down the hall to the door that Miss Thomas said was the bathroom.

When I was done I pulled on a chain that made the water come down. The loud noise made me jump back.

Man, these inside-the-house outhouses were hard to

get used to. I washed my hands with running hot water and closed the bathroom door kind of loud.

I *clump-clump-clump*ed down the steps, stopping a couple of times to yawn real loud.

When I walked into the kitchen they all had looks on their faces like they hadn't been talking about me at all.

I said, "Good morning, Mr. Calloway," but I didn't really mean it, then said, "Good morning, Miss Thomas, good morning, Mr. Jimmy, good morning, Steady Eddie."

I noticed right away that Miss Thomas didn't have all her diamond rings on, I guess it would've been hard sleeping with them flashing lights up at you, she must have to keep them closed up in a box that the sparkles can't get out of. I noticed too that even without the rings Miss Thomas still had to be the most beautiful woman in the world.

They smiled and said, "Good morning, Bud." All except Herman E. Calloway. He got up from the table and said, "I don't like the way Loudean is sounding, I'ma have a look at her plugs."

He went outside through a door at the back of the kitchen.

Miss Thomas said, "Bud, we'd just about given up on you. Do you usually sleep until after noon?"

After noon? Man, I couldn't believe it, I'd slept as long as those rich folks in the moving pictures!

"No, ma'am, that's the first time I ever did that."

She said, "I know you must be starving, but if you can hold out for another half hour or so Mr. Jimmy's going to make everyone's lunch. Think you can wait?"

"Yes, ma'am." A half hour wasn't nothing to wait, no matter how hungry you were.

Mr. Jimmy said, "So what's the scoop, little man?"

I didn't know what that meant so I said, "Nothing, sir."

Steady Eddie said, "How'd you sleep, kiddo?"

"Great, sir." Oops, I forgot I wasn't supposed to call the band men *sir*.

He said, "Cop a squat." He pointed at a chair. I guessed that meant "sit down," so I did.

Miss Thomas said, "Were your ears burning last night, Bud?"

Man, all these Grand Rapids people really do talk funny. I only came from the other side of the state and it was like they talked some strange language out here.

I said, "What, ma'am?"

She said, "There's an old saying that when people talk about you behind your back your ears start to get real warm, kind of like they were burning."

I said, "No, ma'am, my ears felt just fine."

She said, "Well, they should've been burning, you were the subject of a very long conversation last night. But as sound asleep as you were, I'm really not all that surprised you didn't notice. I had to check your pulse to make sure you were still alive!"

Shucks! I knew it. She did come in when I was conked out and took my doggone pants and shirt off and put me there. Man, this was real embarrassing.

Miss Thomas said, "Mr. Calloway and the band and I talked about you for a long time. We've come up with something we want to discuss with you, but we need your help in deciding what to do."

Uh-oh. That was Rules and Things Number 36, or something, that meant I was going to have to get ready to go fetch something for her.

I said, "Yes, ma'am?"

She said, "We've got to talk to some people in Flint first, but if they say it's all right, we were hoping that you'd stay here at Grand Calloway Station for a while."

A gigantic smile split my face in half.

Miss Thomas said, "I'm going to assume that that smile means yes."

I said, "Yes, ma'am! Thank you, ma'am!"

Miss Thomas said, "Before that grin gets stuck on your face, let me tell you you're going to have lots of chores and things to take care of around here, Bud, you'll be expected to pull your own weight the best you can. We all like a very clean house and none of us are too used to having children around, so we're all going to have to learn to be patient with each other. There's one person in particular that you're going to have to be very patient with. Do you know who I mean?"

I sure did. "Yes, ma'am, it's Mr. Calloway."

She said, "Good boy, give him some time. He really needs help with a lot of different things, he swears someone's adding weight onto that bass fiddle of his every year, but he's just getting older. He can use some young, wiry hands to help him around. Think you can handle that?"

Now I knew for sure she'd looked at my legs, she must've thought I was a real weakling.

I said, "Yes, ma'am, my legs are a lot stronger than they look, most folks are surprised by that."

Miss Thomas said, "I don't doubt that at all, Bud. I'm not worried about your body being strong, I'm more concerned about your spirit. Lord knows Mr. Calloway is going to give it a test."

I said, "Yes, ma'am, my spirit's a lot stronger than it looks too, most folks are really surprised by that."

She smiled and said, "Very good, but you know what, Bud?"

"What, ma'am?"

"I knew you were an old toughie the minute I saw you."

I smiled again.

She said, "Our schedule's pretty heavy for the next

couple of months, and then come September we'll have to see about school for you, but we'll be doing a lot of traveling right around Michigan, so I hope you don't mind long car trips."

"No, ma'am."

She said, "That's great, Bud. Something tells me you were a godsend to us, you keep that in mind all of the time, OK?"

"Yes, ma'am."

Then she did something that made me feel strange. She stood up, grabbed both my arms and looked right hard in my face, just like Momma used to, she said, "Really, Bud, I want you to always keep that in mind, this might get hard for you some of the time and I don't always travel with the band, so I don't want you to forget what I'm telling you."

I said, "No, ma'am, I won't."

Steady Eddie said, "Since you're going to be part of the family there're some things we've got to talk about. Now I've noticed the tight grip you keep on that old suitcase of your'n. I need to know how attached to it you are."

"I carry it with me everywhere I go 'cause all my things are in there." I wasn't sure if I liked the way this talk was going.

Steady Eddie said, "That's what I need to know, are you attached to the suitcase, or is it the things inside that are important?"

I'd never thought about that before, I'd always thought of the suitcase and the things inside together.

I said, "The things I got from my mother are the most important."

He said, "Good, 'cause if you're going to be traveling with us it just wouldn't look too copacetic for you to be carrying that ratty old bag."

He reached under the kitchen table and pulled out one of those funny-looking suitcases that the band kept all their instruments in. This one looked like a baby one to his.

He put it on the table, opened it and said, "Since you're going to be traveling with Herman E. Calloway and the Worthy Swarthys, which is known far and wide as a very classy band, it's only fitting that you quit carrying your things in that cardboard suitcase.

"This is my old alto saxophone case, I've been hanging on to it for three years now, ever since the horn got stole right off the stage in Saginaw, but it doesn't look like I'm ever gonna get it back, so I figured you might as well keep your momma's things in it."

Wow! "Thank you, Steady Eddie!"

I pulled my new case over to me. The inside of it had a great big dent where Steady Eddie's saxophone used to go, now there wasn't anything in it but a little raggedy pink towel. The case had some soft smooth black stuff all over the inside of it, it covered everything, even the dent. There was a real old smell that came out of it too, like dried-up slobber and something dead. It smelled great!

The back kitchen door opened and I thought Herman E. Calloway was coming back in to ruin everybody's fun, but it was the rest of the band.

Everybody said hello, poured themselves some coffee, then sat down at the table.

Doo-Doo Bug said, "I see Mr. C.'s got Loudean's carburetor tore down again, anything wrong?"

Miss Thomas said, "There's lots wrong, but not with that car."

They all laughed so I joined in too.

I patted my new case and said, "This here's my case now, I'm going to be going around with you."

They smiled and Dirty Deed said, "So we hear. Glad to have you on board, partner."

Steady Eddie said, "I was just about to tell him some of the things Herman E. Calloway requires of anybody in his band."

The Thug said, "Otherwise known as Herman E. Calloway's Rules to Guarantee You Have No Female Companionship, No Alcohol and No Fun at All."

"Rule number one, practice two hours a day."

Mr. Jimmy said, "That's a good one."

Steady Eddie said, "So I got you this, Bud."

Steady Eddie had another present for me! This was a

long, brown, skinny wooden flute. I was going to have to learn music!

He said, "It's called a recorder. Once you've developed a little wind, and some tone and a embouchure we'll move on to something a little more complicated."

These must've been more of those Grand Rapids words 'cause they sure weren't like any American talk I ever heard before.

I said, "Thank you!"

Steady Eddie said, "Don't thank me until you've been through a couple of hours of blowing scales. We'll see if you're still grateful then."

The Thug said, "Now all that's left is to give little stuff here a name."

Miss Thomas said, "You know, I don't like the way Loudean's been sounding, I think I'm gonna go check the air in the trunk." She picked her coffee up and started to leave the kitchen.

Doo-Doo Bug said, "You don't have to leave, Miss Thomas."

"Darling, I know that, it's just that this is one of those man things that you all think is so mysterious and special that I have absolutely no interest in. The only thing I can hope is that the process has improved since you four were given your names." Then she left the room.

As soon as she was gone Steady Eddie told me, "Hand me your ax and stand up, Bud." I was starting to catch on to this Grand Rapids talk, I remembered that a ax was a instrument. I handed Steady my recorder and stood up in front of him.

He said, "Uh-uh, she was right, this is mysterious and special, so that grin's got to go, brother."

I tried to tie down my smile.

Steady said, "Mr. Jimmy, you're the senior musician here, would you proceed?"

Mr. Jimmy said, "Gentlemen, the floor's open for names for the newest member of the band, Bud-not-Buddy."

They started acting like they were in school. The Thug raised his hand and Mr. Jimmy pointed at him.

Thug said, "Mr. Chairman, in light of the boy's performance last night at the Sweet Pea, I nominate the name Waterworks Willie."

Shucks, I was hoping they'd forgot about that.

Mr. Jimmy said, "You're out of order, Douglas."

Steady raised his hand. "Mr. Chairman, this boy's obviously going to be a musician, he slept until twelve-thirty today, so I propose that we call him Sleepy."

Mr. Jimmy said, "The name Sleepy is before the board, any comments?"

Dirty Deed said, "Too simple. I think we need something that lets folks know about how slim the boy is."

Doo-Doo Bug said, "How about the Bone?"

Steady said, "Not enough class, he needs something so people will know right off that the boy's got class."

Mr. Jimmy said, "How do you say *bone* in French? French always makes things sound a lot classier."

The Thug said, "That's easy, *bone* in French is *la bone*."

Doo-Doo Bug said, "*La bone,* nah, it don't have a ring to it."

Steady Eddie said, "I got it, we'll compromise. How about Sleepy LaBone?"

I couldn't tie the smile down anymore, that was about the best name I'd ever heard in my life!

Mr. Jimmy said, "Let me try it out. Ladies and gentlemen, thank you very much for coming out on this cold November night, this night that will live in history, this night that for the first time on any stage anywhere, you have listened to the smooth saxophonical musings of that prodigy of the reed, Mr. Sleepy LaBone!"

The whole crowd broke out clapping.

The Thug said, "What can I say but *bang!*"

Dirty Deed said, "You nailed him!"

Doo-Doo Bug said, "That is definitely smooth."

Steady said, "My man!"

Mr. Jimmy said, "Kneel down, young man."

I got down on one knee.

Mr. Jimmy tapped me on the head three times with

my recorder and said, "Arise and welcome to the band, Mr. Sleepy LaBone."

I got off my knee and looked at my bandmates.

Sleepy LaBone. Shucks, that was the kind of name that was enough to make you forget folks had ever called you Buddy, or even Clarence. That was the kind of name that was enough to make you practice *four* hours every day, just so you could live up to it!

# CHAPTER 17

*I HELD THE MOP* so that it was floating on the top of the water in the bucket. I was pretending it was that underwater boat in the book Momma read to me, *Twenty Thousand Leaks Under the Sea.*

"Captain Nemo," I whispered, pretending I was a sailor.

"Aye, matey?"

"The squabs were only able to plug ten thousand of the leaks we have, that means we have ten thousand left, and dag-gum-it, I think we're going down with all hands on board!"

I looked up to make sure no one was watching me too close. The Dusky Devastators of the Depression were still putting their instruments on the stage, waiting for Miss Thomas and Mr. Jimmy and Herman E. Calloway.

I whispered, "Heavenly Father, all is lost!" Then I made the mop sink into the water, drowning Captain Nemo, matey, and all the poor squabs. They went down with a bunch of bubbles and soap suds and dirt.

I know Herman E. Calloway was trying to work me like a dog, but he was doing a real bad job at it. I'd already wiped all the tables and chairs down in the Log Cabin and now I was going back to clear-mop the floor for the second time. It was a piece of cake! The bucket even had a thing on top of it that you could use to wring the mop out, and Herman E. Calloway didn't even know how much fun I was having. Making somebody work hard isn't as easy as it looks, some folks are good at it and some folks aren't.

Some folks can look at you and tell if you're even thinking about slacking off, they'll add some work to you faster than you can say Jack Robinson. Some folks will find a excuse to strap you even if you're working as hard as you ever did in your life.

I stuck the mop head into the wringer. I pretended it

was somebody at a washing machine not paying attention to what he was doing and getting his whole body pulled through and wrungeded out.

I let the handle up to see what was left of this poor soul but before I could check, someone yelled out, "One, two, one two three!"

I looked up.

The Thug was brushing his sticks across the round gold metal thing next to his drums and making it sound like a soft rain was commencing to fall on someone's tin roof. Only instead of sounding like rain splashing anytime it wanted to, the Thug had it sounding like it was coming down in a steady, bouncing way.

Then Dirty Deed started making the piano sound like it was a kind of drum, for a second it fell right in with the rain pats that the Thug was making, then it took off and made you think of what Niagara Falls must sound like, it sounded like big, bright drops of water splashing up and over, over and up. The drops would fall loud and clear as anything, then before you knew it they were right back into the Thug's steady, bouncy beat.

Steady Eddie started snapping his fingers real soft, in time with the piano and the drum, his toothpick jumping right along with his fingers. He put his ax in his mouth and blew, but instead of the horn making music it seemed like Steady made it talk. He blew one long, low, rumbly sound and I knew right then, with that one deep, sad moan, what the most beautiful sound in the world was. Steady held the note for a long time, then made the sax drift away from the rest of the storm of music. It swirled and floated back and joined the rain sound that the Thug and Dirty Deed kept going.

I just stood there. I didn't even hear Miss Thomas and Mr. Jimmy and Herman E. Calloway come up from behind me.

Miss Thomas rubbed her hand acrost my head and said, "Bud, you've done a great job, the place is sparkling."

I was going to say, "Thank you, ma'am," but it seemed like talking was wrong what with all these wonderful sounds were coming from the people on the stage.

Mr. Jimmy said, "LaBone, looking good, son."

Herman E. Calloway grunted and the three of them walked up on the stage.

Mr. Jimmy picked up his horn and joined in the storm. Miss Thomas sat on a stool, closed her eyes and ducked her head up and down, up and down. Herman E. Calloway stood next to his giant fiddle and started bobbing his head too. He put one of his hands near the top of the fiddle and began pulling at the strings with his other hand.

Every time he patted the strings it seemed like something wide and heavy was walking by slow and easy. Or it seemed like he was the thunder, soft and far away but getting closer all the time.

All of the instruments blended up together and, just like that smell in the library, you couldn't tell which one was your favorite. First you'd say it was Mr. Jimmy on the trumpet, then Doo-Doo Bug's trombone would make you think it was the best, then Dirty Deed would make the piano sound like water hitting big rocks and you'd know there wasn't anything that sounded that good until Steady Eddie would make the saxophone sing and talk and dance around everyone else and you'd swear that was the only sound you'd ever want to hear again. All the while Herman E. Calloway and the Thug kept everything moving by making the drums and the giant fiddle pound out a soft steady beat, like someone's heart turned way up loud.

You'd have a real hard time trying to figure out which instrument was your favorite. Until Miss Thomas opened her mouth. While the rest of the band was being a storm, she was the sun busting through thick, gray clouds. With the first thing she sang, you had to wonder why this band was called Herman E. Calloway and the Dusky Devastators of the Depression, or Herman E. Calloway and the Nubian Knights, it should be called Miss Thomas and the Dusky Devastators of the Depression and a Mean Old Guy on the Giant Fiddle.

She was so good she didn't even have to sing real words, mostly she was saying things like "La da de da de da da, ha whee a ho, ha whee a ho, ha whee a day," then Steady Eddie would answer on the saxophone and before you knew it, the two of them were having a regular conversation.

Every once in a while Mr. Jimmy's trumpet would come in and put his two cents' worth in, then it would fade away. All the other instruments took turns trying to interrupt the conversation, but in the end it was Miss Thomas's voice and Steady's saxophone doing the talking that you really wanted to listen to.

Finally Miss Thomas did a bunch more "Doe de doe de doe de bahs" and Steady answered, then, just when you thought you could understand this language they were talking, Miss Thomas broke out in American, she sang,

"We haven't met since then, gee, but it's nice to see you again," she said, "nice to see you, to see you again," and the storm was over. The last thing you could hear was the rain from the Thug and the thunder from Herman E. Calloway getting farther and farther away, like the storm had gone and blowed itself over into the next county.

Then it was dead quiet. I let the mop fall over and clapped as loud as I could and said, "Wow!"

Miss Thomas stood up and did one of those curtsey bows.

I clapped louder. I could see now why this band got to have six exclamation points behind their name!

# CHAPTER 18

*WE GOT IN TWO CARS* to drive for a hour and a half north of Grand Rapids. We were headed to a dinky town called Mecosta. I got to ride with the band while Mr. Jimmy and Herman E. Calloway and the instruments were riding in the Packard. Miss Thomas stayed back at Grand Calloway Station. I'd been living with Miss Thomas and the band for about seven days and this was already my third trip on the road.

The band was doing their next favorite thing to playing

music, they were teasing each other and talking about Herman E. Calloway behind his back.

The Thug said to Dirty Deed, "I'd be offended, man, and I ain't trying to say that you ain't good on the eighty-eights, but you know the only reason you got this gig is 'cause you're Dutch, you're white and you don't have the strongest personality in the world."

Deed said, "Yeah, well, such is life. You think I'm going to give up the best gig in the state just 'cause you'd be offended? Take a look out the window, baby, there's a depression going on. How many folks you see living like us, Negro or white? Not many. That man may have his faults but he's a struggler, I'm putting my hat in with him."

Eddie looked at me and said, "Bud, Mr. C. has always got a white fella in the band, for practical reasons. But we don't hold his skin color against him, he can't help that he was born that way."

Deed said, "You're just too kind, Edward."

Eddie kept talking, "We do that 'cause the boy can play, Mr. C. won't compromise on his music."

I said, "Why does he always keep one white guy in the band?"

Deed said, "It's the way of the world, Sleepy. It's against the law for a Negro to own any property out where the Log Cabin is so Mr. C. put it in my name."

Eddie said, "That, and a lot of times we get gigs playing

polkas and waltzes and a lot of these white folks wouldn't hire us if they knew we were a Negro band so Deed goes out and sets up everything."

"But what do they say when the Dusky Devastators show up?"

Deed said, "Well, it's too late for them to say anything then, it's us or no music."

Eddie said, "And Mr. C. tells them if we aren't the best band they'd ever had then they don't have to pay. We haven't been stiffed yet."

With all the arguing and jokes about Mr. C., the trip seemed real short. We unloaded all of the instruments and waited for nighttime to come.

I'd heard the band play and practice a thousand times and still had to just about sit on my hands when they were finished so I wouldn't bust out clapping.

We finished our set at a little place called the Laughing Jackass and I got to sleep right onstage to guard the instruments. The next morning I was packing everything into the cases when I got some real bad news.

Herman E. Calloway told Mr. Jimmy, "I'ma stay and catch up with Eugene, you head back with the boys." The man who owned the club, Mr. Eugene Miller, used to be in one of Mr. C.'s bands.

Mr. Jimmy said, "Bud, take your time loading everything into the Packard and you can ride back with Herman."

Uh-oh. Me and Mr. C. looked at each other like this wasn't a good idea. He said, "Whatever," and walked back to the club's office.

Shucks, a whole hour and a half trapped in a car with him.

I loaded all of the instruments into the Packard, sat on a big rock and took out my recorder to practice. I could hear Mr. C. and Mr. Miller talking and laughing for the longest time.

At last Herman E. Calloway came out and walked over to the side of the building and started nudging things around with the toe of his shoe. I walked over to watch what he was doing.

When I got next to him I could see that it was just rocks he was pushing around. Finally he grunted a couple of times and started to bend over but his big belly got in the way and wouldn't let his arms reach to the ground. After a bunch more grunts he said, "Make yourself useful, boy, and hand me this one."

"This what, sir?"

"This stone, this one."

Right at the end of Mr. C.'s shiny brown shoe was a little roundish rock. I bent over to pick it up, blew some dirt off of it and turned it over a couple of times in my hand to try and see why Mr. C. thought it was so special. The only thing that I could tell was that he'd picked a perfect throwing rock, the exact same kind of rock I'd use if I was about to chunk someone in the head. I dropped it into his hand.

He didn't look at it or nothing, he just stuck it in his pocket and I heard it bang up against some silver dollars.

I kept my nose out of his business for as long as I could then had to say, "Mr. C., wasn't that just a rock?"

"Sure was." He started walking back to the Packard. I followed.

There were a million ways to ask what I wanted to know and I chose the worst one when I said, "What in Sam Hill are you going to do with a doggone rock?" It sounded a lot meaner than I wanted it to but I was really surprised that Mr. C. would want a old rock.

He climbed in on one side of the Packard and I climbed in on the other. After he stuck the key in the dashboard he said, "Bad habit."

Then he leaned over toward me and opened the glove box of the car. There weren't any gloves or maps or papers in the box, just a bunch of perfect throwing rocks. They all looked like they had writing on them.

I reached in and took one of the rocks out. Written on the back of it was "idlewild m. 5.2.36." I took another one and it said "preston in. 6.4.36." These were just like my rocks! I took one more and it said, "chicago il. 3.19.32."

I looked over to Mr. C. and said, "I've got some of these, sir."

He said, "Hmmm."

"Really, I've got some too."

He looked at me, shifted his pipe away from the talking side of his mouth and said, "Bud, I know you're not the sharpest knife in the drawer, and I hate to be the bearer of bad tidings, but those are found all over the world. In fact, they're about as common as rocks."

I almost didn't answer him but since I didn't want to look so stupid I said, "Yes, sir, but mine have writing and numbers on them too."

He said, "Hmmm."

We kept driving. Finally I said to him, "You don't believe me, I'll show you."

I dropped his three rocks back into the glove box and closed it, then climbed over the front seat to get at my sax case. I found it and set it on the backseat and unlocked it. As soon as I opened the top that smell of old spit and crumbling-up velvet and mildew came rushing out, it was still great. I lifted the little door that covered my rocks and took two of them out. I climbed back over the front seat but kept the rocks covered in my hand—if he was going to see these he was going to have to ask first. I crossed my arms across my chest and waited.

It's a good thing I've got lots of patience 'cause I waited a long, long time.

When we finally got back to Grand Calloway Station Mr. Jimmy helped us unload the car.

Finally I decided that Mr. C. had waited long enough. I stuck my rocks in his face and said, "See, I told you I had some rocks like those, the only difference is mine say, 'flint m dot eight dot eleven dot eleven' and 'gary in dot six dot thirteen dot twelve.' "

He said, "Where did you find these? Didn't I tell you not to do any rummaging around in that room you been sleeping in?"

He reached for the rocks. I don't know why, but I let him take them. He was the first person other than Bugs that I'd ever let touch the rocks that my momma had give to me.

Mr. C. turned the rocks over and over in his hands and said, "Well? Where'd you get these?"

Uh-oh, I could tell by the way Herman E. Calloway was holding my rocks that he didn't plan on giving them back to me anytime soon. I kept watching his hand, waiting for a chance to snatch my rocks and get out of there.

If I could get my hands back on my rocks I knew I could outrun Mr. C. even though he was a lot stronger and his legs were a lot longer than mine.

Herman E. Calloway said, "Answer me, where'd you take these from?"

Mr. C. sounded meaner than he ever had before. Mr. Jimmy heard him and put down the box he was carrying and walked over to us real quick.

Herman E. Calloway had the rocks squeezed tight in his right-hand fist and had his left-hand fist balled up like he was ready to fight.

Mr. Jimmy said, "Herman? What's this? What's wrong?" He stood between me and Mr. C.

Herman E. Calloway said, "I told you about this boy from the word go. He's been snooping through things in the house that he's got no business being in, he stole these."

I said, "No, sir, I did not."

Mr. C. said, "Then where'd you get them? I'm not going to ask you again." He unsqueezed the rocks in his hand. I was surprised they hadn't turned into diamonds or dust the way he'd been holding them so tight.

Mr. Jimmy took my two rocks from him. He looked at the writing and said, "Flint, Michigan, August eighth, 1911, and Gary, Indiana, July thirteenth, 1912? That's more than twenty-five years ago."

He squatted down and looked right at me and said, "Son, where'd you find these? Just tell the truth."

I kept one eye on Mr. C., he still looked like he was getting ready to jump funny on me.

I said, "Mr. Jimmy, I didn't find them or steal them from nowhere, these've always been mine. I got them from my momma and that's the swear-'fore-God truth. Now could I please have my rocks back, sir?" I stuck my hand out.

Both Mr. Jimmy and Herman E. Calloway said, "Your momma?"

"Yes, sir." I kept my hand out.

Mr. Jimmy said, "Bud, where did your mother get these?"

I said, "I don't know, sir. She always had them."

Mr. Jimmy and Herman E. Calloway were looking at me with that can't-decide-which-hand-to-smack-you-with-look when Mr. Jimmy said, "Bud, what did you say your momma's name was?"

"No one ever asked me, sir."

Herman E. Calloway was still hot. "You throw a lot of 'sirs' around but you've still got a real strong, real smart-mouthed, disrespectful streak in you, boy. Now you answer the question or I'll—"

I screamed at him, "Angela, sir." I was so mad that I hadn't meant to say "sir" but it came out anyway. "Her name is Angela Janet Caldwell."

Mr. Jimmy said, "Lord have mercy. . . ."

Herman E. Calloway's pipe dropped out of his mouth and he stumbled and fumbled into Grand Calloway Station, feeling his way like he'd been struck blind.

Then I knew! Herman E. Calloway *was* the best liar in the world, he'd been lying to me and everybody else all along! Now that there was some good proof against him he was all shook up.

I said to Mr. Jimmy, "I knew it! I knew he was my father!"

Mr. Jimmy was still crouched down right in front of me. He said, "Bud, he's not your father."

"Yes, sir, he is. That's why he run off like that, he got caught lying after all these years!"

Mr. Jimmy said, "Bud, that's enough. Herman is *not* your father. But Angela Janet is his daughter's name. If what you're saying is true, Lord help us all, it looks like Herman might be your grandfather."

This was real surprising, but the thing I felt most was glad that Herman E. Calloway wasn't my dad. Shucks, who'd want a daddy that on top of being so old and so doggone mean had such a big belly? Not me.

# CHAPTER 19

*MAN!* Ever since he heard me call my momma's name Herman E. Calloway had locked hisself up in his room and wouldn't come out.

Mr. Jimmy and Miss Thomas made me sit at the kitchen table whilst they knocked on his door and tried to talk him into opening it up, but the way they kept saying "Herman" soft at first, then louder and louder, it sounded like he wasn't talking back. After the longest while they decided to let the big baby have his own way and came back downstairs. They sat at the kitchen table with me.

Miss Thomas looked at me and said, "My, my, my."

Mr. Jimmy said, "Now look here, Bud." He wiped his hand over his face. "You're sure your momma's name was Angela Janet?"

I said, "Yes, sir."

"And the two of you both had the same last name, her last name was Caldwell too, she never said nothing about being no Calloway?"

I spelt it out for him. "No, sir, her name was Caldwell, C-A-L-D-W-E-L-L."

It seemed like he finally believed me, he said, "OK, OK, I hope you don't mind me asking, Bud, but it's pretty important that we know, how'd your momma pass? And how long ago was it?"

*Pass* was just like *gone,* it was another one of those words grown folks use instead of *dead.*

I said, "I was six years old when it happened, sir. I don't know why, she was too sick to go to work for six days in a row, then one morning I went into her room and she was dead. But she didn't suffer or nothing, it happened real quick, she didn't even have time to close her eyes, she didn't look like it hurt or nothing."

Miss Thomas reached across the table and touched my arm, she said, "I'm sure it didn't, Bud, I'm sure it was very peaceful for her."

Mr. Jimmy said, "When she was living, Bud, God rest her soul, what'd your momma look like?"

This was another strange question, but before I could

answer, Miss Thomas said, "James, what are you insinuating? I knew there was something familiar about this boy, I don't know how I missed it before but look at Bud's eyes, you have to ask if this is Herman's grandchild?"

Mr. Jimmy said, "Now hold on, Grace, I'm just trying to ask the questions I know Herman'd ask if he could. Ain't a thing wrong with being certain before we jump to any conclusions. Now what'd she look like, son?"

I said, "She was real pretty, sir."

Mr. Jimmy said, "I bet she was, Bud, but that ain't what I meant. Was she short or tall, was she slim or bigboned?"

I said, "I don't know, sir, she was real pretty and real tall and kind of skinny like me, I guess."

Miss Thomas said, "James, Bud was six years old, everyone on earth was real tall to him. I don't see the point in all this."

I said, "Pardon me, ma'am, I know how I can show you what she looks like, I still got her picture."

They just stared at me.

I said, "Can I be excused?"

Miss Thomas said, "Yes, son, hurry up and go get that picture."

I busted up the stairs but stopped like I hit a brick wall. I remembered how mad and crazy Herman E. Calloway looked when he yelled at me. I tippytoed up the rest of the steps.

Uh-oh! Herman E. Calloway's door was opened up a crack!

I held my breath and tiptoed extra quiet and extra fast right into the little dead girl's room and as soon as I did . . . woop, zoop, sloop . . . my heart jumped down into my stomach.

Herman E. Calloway was sitting on the little chair in front of the little mirror on the dressing table. His elbows were on the table and his face was covered by his hands. It sounded like he was having trouble breathing 'cause every time he sucked in a bunch of air he made a sound like "Mu-u-u-u-h . . ." and every time he blew air out he made a sound like, "H-u-u-u-h . . ."

I didn't know what to do. I could tell Mr. C. didn't know I was in the room with him so I could probably just backward tiptoe and get out of there without anything happening.

I rose up on my toes, took two baby steps back and stopped. Shucks, I'd come up here to show Miss Thomas and Mr. Jimmy what my momma looked like, there wasn't nothing wrong with that, I wasn't doing nothing that meant I had to sneak out of this room on my tiptoes going backwards.

I sucked in a mouthful of air and walked over to my bed. I picked up my sax case and set it on top of the bed.

I pushed the two silver buttons to the side and the two silver tongues jumped open and made those loud *click-click* sounds. Herman E. Calloway still didn't take his face out of his hands. He kept going, "Muh . . . huh . . . muh . . . huh . . . muh . . . huh . . ."

I reached inside my sax case and took out the envelope with Momma's picture in it. I closed the two silver tongues again and could tell that Mr. C. wasn't paying me no mind at all, he kept his face in his hands, his head was rocking up and down real slow, sort of like he was checking to see how much it weighed.

I put my sax case back next to the bed and was about to leave the room when I looked over at Herman E. Calloway's back.

He still didn't know I was in the room with him. I looked in the little round mirror and still couldn't see his face, but I could see his hands a lot better. I could see six little trails of water coming out from where his fingers joined up with his hands, the three trails from each hand joined up together on his wrists and ran down his arms puddling up on top of the dressing table.

Shucks, Herman E. Calloway was bawling his eyes out. He was acting like me being his grandson was the worst news anyone could ever give you in your life.

This was Number 39 of Bud Caldwell's Rules and Things to Have a Funner Life and Make a Better Liar Out of Yourself.

## RULES AND THINGS NUMBER 39

### The Older You Get, the Worse
### Something Has to Be to Make You Cry.

With babies it's easy not to pay them no mind 'cause crying's just like talking for a baby. A baby's tears might mean, "Hey! You just stuck a pin in my behind when you changed my diapers," or their crying might be the way they picked out to say, "Good morning, Momma, what're we gonna do today?" That makes it easy not to care too much about a baby's tears.

When you got a old person crying you got a whole 'nother story. When you got someone as old as Herman E. Calloway crying you better look around, 'cause you know you're square in the middle of one of those boiling tragedies. You can't help but feel sorry for him, even if he's been mean to you from the minute he first laid eyes on you, even if he's crying 'cause he found out the two of you were kin.

I walked over to Herman E. Calloway and before I could think my hand moved out toward his back. I waited for one of those spaces between the *muh*s and the *huh*s, then I touched him. His skin under his shirt was very, very warm.

It took a second for Herman E. Calloway to know someone was touching him. When he knew, I felt his skin jerk and twitch the same way a horse's does when a fly lands on it. He whipped his head around.

When he saw it was me he jerked away, took one more giant *huh,* then stared. His mouth started moving like he was talking in a secret language that only dogs could hear.

At last real American words started coming out of his mouth.

He said, "I . . . I . . . how'd . . . I'm, I'm so . . . look, Buddy . . . I . . . I just . . ."

"It's Bud, sir, not Buddy."

He put his face back in his hands and broke down all over again.

Man, it's a good thing the Thug wasn't around, 'cause if he'd've heard the way Mr. C. was weeping, no one would've wondered who the real Waterworks Willie was.

I put my hand back on Mr. C.'s shoulder and patted him and rubbed him a couple of times, then left the room. It felt a lot better going out frontwards instead of sneaking out backwards.

I ran down the steps back into the kitchen. Miss Thomas's and Mr. Jimmy's eyes jumped right onto my envelope. I set it in the middle of the table.

Both of them just looked at it before Miss Thomas reached out and picked it up. She went into the pocket of her dress and took some funny little glasses that only had a bottom half to them, then put them on her nose. She pulled Momma's picture out and held it as far away from her eyes as her arms would stretch.

She looked at the picture, looked over her glasses at me, then looked right at Mr. Jimmy and said, "Any more questions for this young man?" She slid the picture over to him.

Mr. Jimmy picked it up and said, "Well, I'll be, remember that old con man who used to drag that ruint horse through town, now what was his name? Help me out here, Grace, didn't he call his act Joey Pegus and his Broke-Back Broncking Bucko?"

Miss Thomas said, "It was Joey Pegus and his Broke-Back Bucking Bronco, James. What else do you see in the picture?"

Mr. Jimmy said, "Uh, uh, uh, that definitely is Angela Janet Calloway!"

He looked at me and said, "You sure this is your mother?"

I said, "Yes, sir. But her name's Caldwell, not Calloway."

He said, "Well, I'll just be—"

Miss Thomas butted in on him. "There's little doubt about that, James, but what we've got to do . . ."

She kept on talking but I quit listening 'cause something just came out of the blue and give me a good whop right on my forehead. Without even thinking about what

I was doing, I butted in on Miss Thomas and said, "That means that's not some little dead girl's room I'm sleeping in, that's my momma's room!"

She looked at me kind of surprised, like this was the first time she'd had that thought too, she said, "That's right, Bud, you're back in your momma's room."

I said, "How come Herman E. Calloway never called on me and my mother? All he'd've had to do was call on us one time and I know she wouldn't have been so sad."

Miss Thomas and Mr. Jimmy took turns shooting quick looks at each other, then she said, "Bud, give me your hand."

Uh-oh, pretty soon I'd have to come up with a Rules and Things about when Miss Thomas holds your hand.

She stretched her arm across the table and I held on to her fingers.

"Bud," she said, "Mr. C.—excuse me, your granddad didn't know anything about you. No one knew where your mother had gone."

Mr. Jimmy said, "That's right, son, she just up and run off one day. I mean we all knew Herman was hard on her, but it wasn't like it was nothing personal, he was hard on everybody. I used to tell him all the time to slack off some on the girl, to go easy, but I can remember his exact words, he said, 'Easy-go don't make the mare run. This is a hard world, especially for a Negro woman, there's a hundred million folks out there of every shade and hue, both male and female, who are just dying to be harder on her than I ever could be. She's got to be ready.' Shoot, I could see that the girl wasn't the type to—"

Miss Thomas said, "James, why don't you go up and check on Herman." She said "why don't you," but it wasn't a question.

Mr. Jimmy said, "Oh. Oh, maybe I should," and left the kitchen.

Miss Thomas told me, "Bud, I know you can see your granddad has troubles getting along with most folks, right?"

"Yes, ma'am."

"I think it's because he expects so much out of everybody, himself included. And when you set your standards so high, you get let down a lot."

I shook my head up and down, acting like I understood.

She said, "Now take your mother, for instance. He was so, so proud of that young woman, and he loved her very, very much. He was determined that she was going to be the first Calloway to get schooling all the way through college so he thought he had to be strict on her, but he went overboard, Bud, simple as that. He used to crow about how his mother and father had been born slaves and how now it was only two generations later and the Calloways had come so far and worked so hard that one of them was actually going to be a teacher.

"It was his dream, not hers—not yet, anyway—and

he never gave her time to pick it for herself. The more he pushed her, the more she fought him. Finally it got to be too much and she left. We think she ran off with one of Herman's drummers.

"We've been hoping for eleven years that she'd send word or come home, and she finally has. Looks to me like she sent us the best word we've had in years."

Miss Thomas smiled at me and I knew she was trying to say I was the word that my momma had sent to them.

She said, "Wait here for one second, precious. I've got to go to my room for something."

Miss Thomas was probably saying that as a excuse so she could blow her nose and cry, but she came back in a flash. She was holding a iron picture frame and handed it to me.

"This has been on my dressing table for thirteen years, Bud, ever since your mother was sixteen years old. Now it belongs to you."

I wanted to say thank you, but I just stared at the picture in the heavy iron frame. It was Momma.

The picture only showed her head, all around the edges it was smoky or foggy so's that it looked like Momma'd poked her head out of a cloud. And Momma was smiling. The same soft smile she'd give me when she got home from work. It'd been so long since I'd seen Momma smile that I wanted to laugh and cry at the same time.

Miss Thomas said, "Let me show you something, Bud."

She took the frame out of my hands and said, "Watch this."

She moved the picture up and down, right and left, then around in circles.

"Do you see how her eyes are on you all the time? No matter which way you look at the picture, she's watching."

It seemed like Momma was looking direct at me no matter where Miss Thomas put the picture.

"I can keep this?"

"I feel like I've been holding on to it until the rightful owner came along, and it looks to me like he's finally shown up. What took you so long, child?"

Miss Thomas patted me underneath my chin.

She said, "But Bud, we've got a problem I'm going to need your help with."

Uh-oh.

"You said you were six years old when your mother died?"

"Yes, ma'am."

"OK, so that was four years ago."

"Yes, ma'am."

"You can remember how bad you felt when you first knew she was gone, can't you?"

"Yes, ma'am." 'Cause it still feels the same.

"Well, you've had four years to try to heal that scar, but it still hurts some of the time, doesn't it?"

"Sometimes a lot."

"I know, Bud. But remember, your grandfather and I just found out that she passed. The hurt is brand-new for us." Miss Thomas started swallowing.

"And even though he hasn't seen her in eleven years, I know there isn't a day that goes by that he doesn't think about her. He'd never admit it, but there isn't one show that we give that he doesn't first look out into the audience, not to see how big the crowd is, but hoping that she'll be out there. Hoping that she'd've seen a flyer tacked to a telephone pole somewhere and would stop by to see him. He loved her so much, Bud. Sorry, sweetheart." She took the hand she wasn't squeezing my fingers with and took out a handkerchief and blew her nose.

"Those stones that he picks up everywhere he performs are for her. She must've been four or five years old, the band was getting ready to travel to Chicago for a week and before we left he asked her what she wanted him to bring back for her. He was thinking a doll or a dress or something, but she told him, 'A wock, Daddy, bring me back a wock from Chicago.' So everywhere we went after that he'd have to get her a 'wock,' he'd write the city and the day we were there on them for her. He's got boxes of them upstairs, eleven years' worth.

"So, Bud, I don't know how Herman is going to be

feeling after this, that's where I need your help. You've got to remember that both Herman and I love your mother just as much as you do."

This didn't seem like it could be true, not just because it didn't seem like anyone could love my mother as much as I do, but because it didn't seem like Herman E. Calloway could love anyone at all.

Miss Thomas said, "So if you can remember, Bud, be patient with him. That ornery old man upstairs is very, very hurt right now and I just can't say where he's going to land after this news gets through blowing him around." Miss Thomas was starting to do that sting-y-eyed blinking.

"So we're going to have to give him some time, we're going to have to let him find out how he feels before—"

Mr. Jimmy came into the kitchen. "Grace," he said, "he wants you." Herman E. Calloway was making everybody feel like they had the blues, it looked like Mr. Jimmy'd just wiped some tears from his eyes too.

Miss Thomas came around to my side of the table and gave me a hug. She said, "You OK?"

I said, "Yes, ma'am."

She said, "Should I go see how he's doing?"

"Yes, ma'am."

She left the kitchen and Mr. Jimmy went into the living room.

I picked Momma's picture up and put it back in the envelope. Mr. C. chose a good name for his house 'cause not a second went by before the back door came open and the Dusky Devastators of the Depression walked in, talking like it was going out of style. As soon as they saw me they all got quiet.

Doo-Doo Bug said, "Hey, Sleepy LaBone, where's everyone at?"

I didn't want to embarrass anyone by saying that all the grown folks were sitting all over the house sobbing their eyes out, so I said, "They're around." I remembered not to call the band "sir."

Steady said, "Well, it's you we wanted anyway." He put a old cardboard suitcase on the table and said, "I told the fellas how hard you've been hitting that recorder and how proud I was of you, so we put a couple of nickels together"—he acted like he was yelling into the other room—"and Lord knows on the peanuts we get it was a real sacrifice." He slapped some skin with Dirty Deed, then started talking regular again. "Anyway, the Thug saw something at the pawnshop and we picked it up for you."

"Can I open it?"

The Thug said, "Well, if you don't, I don't know who will."

Eddie slid the cardboard suitcase over to in front of me. It looked worse than the one I used to carry around, one of the snaps on it was busted clean off and the other one was stuck.

Steady Eddie said, "It's what's inside that's interesting. Just pull on that snap real hard."

I pulled on the snap and it came off right in my hand.

The Thug said, "I knew it, the boy's just too country, he ain't used to handling fine merchandise. We should've give it to him in a paper bag."

I opened the suitcase. Whatever it was was wrapped up in crinkly, wrinkly newspapers.

I started pulling newspapers off and could tell that their gift was real heavy. All of a sudden a shiny piece of gold showed through. I snatched more paper off and couldn't believe my eyes! The Dusky Devastators of the Depression had put their money together and had bought me a baby-size horn like Steady Eddie's saxophone!

Steady Eddie could see I was stuck so he lifted it out of the suitcase and fished around in the bag for the mouthpiece, the neck and the reed holder. He sucked the reed for a minute, put the horn together, then played it.

Man! My horn sounded great!

Eddie said, "It's an alto, Bud, there's a little rust in some of the seams, but that's to be expected with a horn this old. It's still got a good tone to it, this dent didn't throw her off too much." He showed me a big dent on the bottom part of my saxophone. "I repadded, refelted and resprung it. The rest is up to you." He reached in his pocket and took out a can that said BRASSO on the side. "Get you a rag and shine her up. A man should polish his own horn."

I looked at my bandmates and said, "Thank you, thank you very, very much. I'll practice on this so much that I'll be just as good as you guys are in about three weeks!"

Doo-Doo Bug said, "Ohhh, now that's cold."

I said, "Really! I will."

The band laughed so I did too.

Eddie said, "Well, Mr. LaBone, I'll tell you what, since you're so hot to get in this band, I'd better get you started on your lessons right away." He pulled a big silver watch that was tied up to a long chain out of his pocket and said, "I'm going by Tyla's for a while now, but I'll be back around seven. If you've got your ax polished up by then, I'll bring some sheet music along and we can get started, sound good?" His toothpick jumped with each word.

"Sounds great, Steady!"

Eddie took the strap off his neck and handed it to me. I put it on and Eddie handed me my saxophone for the very first time. It was the perfect weight!

I said, "Can I be excused?"

Dirty Deed said, "What, you ain't gonna blow us some notes? We want to hear what you got, Mr. Three-Weeks-from-Now."

I said, "I'll let you hear me in three weeks when we're all on the stage together."

They laughed again and the Thug said, "I'ma let you in on something, Sleepy LaBone, there's certain members of this band that you *will* be outplaying in three weeks, but it's gonna take you a whole lot longer to top me. On the real tip, it's gonna take you at least ten years before you'll be able to even hold my drumsticks."

Steady Eddie said, "Yeah, and that's about nine years and ten months longer than you'll be with the band, Thug."

The Thug said, "Awww, man, you ain't gonna start that up again, you gotta let me know what you heard."

I said, "Can I be excused?"

Eddie said, "Go 'head on, Sleepy LaBone, I'll be back."

I told my bandmates, "Thank you again, thank you very much."

The Thug said, "Nothing to it, little man."

Dirty Deed said, "Now don't let that horn whip you, son."

Doo-Doo Bug said, "Our pleasure, Sleepy."

Steady Eddie said, "Man, get outta here."

I picked up both of Momma's pictures, my horn and the can of Brasso and ran up the stairs.

When I got upstairs I saw that Herman E. Calloway's

door was still open a crack. Miss Thomas's door was closed now and I could hear the two of them in her room talking real soft to each other. I could've stood outside the door and listened if I wanted to but that would've been rude, besides I didn't know for sure how long it would take me to polish up my new horn!

I went into my mother's room and put my sax on the bed that Momma used to sleep in when she was a little girl. I put her smiling picture on the dressing table, then reached under her bed and pulled my sax case out again. I snapped the two silver snaps and started taking out all of my things.

I took my old blanket out and remade my bed with it. I wasn't going to need to carry it around with me anymore. I opened the tobacco pouch and took out the rock that said Flint on it and set it on the bed. I took the pouch and the flyers and walked down the hall to Herman E. Calloway's room. Even though I could still hear him and Miss Thomas talking and boo-hooing in her room, I knocked on his door anyway. When no one answered I opened it.

He had one of those dressing tables with a mirror stuck on the back of it too, so I walked real quick over to it and set the flyers and the bag of four rocks down. I got out of his room as fast as I could.

Whew! Even though it was me who'd carried them around for all these years, you'd have to be a pretty big liar if you'd say those rocks and flyers really belonged to me. Herman E. Calloway's name was all over the flyers and his writing was all over the rocks.

Besides, the way he'd looked so shook up when he saw those rocks for the first time I figure they meant more to him than they did to me anyway.

I went back over to Momma's dressing table and opened the little drawer. I took one of the thumbtacks out and went back to Momma's bed. Next I took out the envelope that had her picture in it. I took out the picture of her riding the sad, saggy pony.

I still couldn't see what she was so unhappy about, the Miss B. Gotten Moon Park looked like somewhere you could have a lot of fun.

I poked the thumbtack into the top of Momma's picture and walked to the wall that she'd stuck all the pictures of horses on. I put Momma right amongst all those ponies and horses she liked so much.

I didn't need to carry that doggone picture around, this wasn't how I remembered Momma anyway, Momma was always excited and jumpy, not sad and poky like this little girl. Momma was kind of old when I met her too, she wasn't young like this picture at all.

The picture looked like it belonged. It's strange the way things turn out, here I'd been carrying Momma around for all this time and I'd finally put her somewhere where she wanted to be, back in her own bedroom, back amongst all her horses.

I went back to the bed and picked the Flint rock up. It

was going to be enough. I didn't need those other things with me all of time. I didn't need them to remind me of Momma, I couldn't think about her any more if there were a hundred hours in every day and a thousand days in every week. I couldn't think of my momma any better than I already do. All I have to do is remember her hand on my forehead when she'd ask me something like, "Baby, are you sick? Have you got a temperature?" All I have to do is remember Momma letting me dry the dishes after she'd wash them, how she used to say no one in the world could dry a plate the way I could. All I have to do is take two or three deep breaths and think of all the books she'd read to me at night, and remember that no matter how long it took she'd read until I went to sleep.

Deza Malone was right, I was carrying Momma inside me and there wasn't anyone or anything that could take away from that or add to it either.

The one rock from Flint would be enough. I set it in my sax case.

I picked up my saxophone. It was the most beautiful thing I'd ever seen!

I wet the reed the same way I'd seen Steady Eddie do, then clamped it on the mouthpiece. I closed my eyes and counted to ten. If after I got to ten I blew the horn and it sounded pretty good I knew I'd be playing along with the Dusky Devastators of the Depression in a week or two. If I didn't sound so good it meant I'd have to practice for a couple of months before I'd be good enough to get onstage with them.

One, two, three, four, five, six, seven, eight, nine, ten!

I puffed my cheeks and blew as hard as I could. The saxophone only squeaked, squawked and groaned, then sounded like it was making up words like *ahwronk* and *roozahga* and *baloopa.*

Shucks, maybe I didn't puff my cheeks out right, maybe I was blowing too hard. I counted again.

One, two, three, four, five, six, seven, eight, nine, ten!

This time the horn only squeaked, squawked and groaned, it didn't sound like it was trying to make up any words. It sounded great! It wasn't perfect, like when Steady blew it, but I could tell that one day it was going to be. Something told me I could learn how to play this. Something told me that those sounds were more than just bad notes.

If you didn't have a real good imagination you'd probably think those noises were the sounds of some kid blowing a horn for the first time, but I knew better than that. I could tell those were the squeaks and squawks of one door closing and another one opening.

I looked at the picture of Momma that Miss Thomas gave me. Momma was looking right at me with that same soft smile. I know it's stupid to smile back at a picture but I couldn't help myself. I know it's even stupider to talk to a picture, especially when it hadn't said anything to start a conversation, but I had to say, "Here we go again, Momma, only this time I can't wait!"

I closed my eyes and began practicing.

Shucks, as good as things were going for me now I'd bet you dollars to doughnuts that Steady Eddie was going to get here early.

# Afterword

ALTHOUGH BUD, NOT BUDDY is fictional, many of the situations Bud encounters are based on events that occurred in the 1930s, during a time known as the Great Depression. And although the characters in *Bud, Not Buddy* are fictional as well, some of them too are based on real people. One of the most enjoyable parts of writing is that an author can combine his or her imagination with the traits of real people to build new characters. That is what I did to create the characters of Lefty Lewis and Herman E. Calloway, both of whom are based loosely on my grandfathers.

My mother's father, Earl "Lefty" Lewis, was one of six or seven redcaps who worked at the train station in Grand Rapids, Michigan, during much of the depression. The jobs of Pullman porter and redcap were among the few open to African American men at that time and carried a certain prestige in the black community. Nonetheless, they were extremely difficult jobs, often marked by eighty-hour workweeks, low salary and virtually no job security. These men could be fired for simply not looking happy enough.

Grandpa Lewis did exceptionally well during the depression, supporting his family on the tips he received as a redcap. My mother remembers that my grandmother used to have to sew reinforced linings into the pockets of all Grandpa's pants because the weight of the pennies, nickels, dimes and occasional quarters that he was given as tips would eventually rip the seams out. She also remembers the leathery texture Grandpa's hands took on from carrying so much baggage at the station.

As the depression deepened, the Grand Rapids train station cut back to two redcaps, and Grandpa was let go. He briefly opened a small restaurant and finally became the first African American cabdriver in Grand Rapids, a job he held until his retirement in 1972 at seventy-four years old.

Earl "Lefty" Lewis also pitched for many years in the

minors of the Negro Baseball Leagues. His fondest memory of that time was pitching twice against Satchel Paige. As he did with most opposing pitchers, Satch hung Grandpa with two losses.

My father's father, Herman E. Curtis, was indeed a big bandleader for most of his adult life. He headed many different musical groups, my favorite being Herman E. Curtis and the Dusky Devastators of the Depression!!!!!!—a name that by itself deserves all six of those exclamation points! Grandpa attended the Indiana Conservatory of Music and was a classically trained violinist. He also played the bass fiddle, the accordion and the piano.

Entertainment was an important part of life during the depression, for people wanted to forget their troubles by going to the movies, sitting around the radio, and listening and dancing to live music. Grandpa and his bands were well known throughout Michigan during this time.

Being an orchestra leader was Grandpa Curtis's night job. By day he wore many different hats, among them those of a chauffeur, boat captain, and truck painter. He owned several businesses in Grand Rapids and Wyoming, Michigan, at a time when laws prohibited African Americans from renting or holding title to land in these two cities. Grandpa did this by having a white friend put his name on all records.

The flexibility, people skills, hustle and willingness to work around unfair laws and situations that both of my

*Above:*
*Herman E. Curtis and the Dusky Devastators of the Depression !!!!!!*
*Herman is at left, with the bow.*

*Opposite: Earl "Lefty" Lewis, pitcher for the Grand Rapids, Michi-*
*gan, Elsterites, taken May 30, 1918*

grandfathers used allowed them to keep their families together during one of America's bleakest periods, a time that was especially hard on African Americans. Both of these men were fortunate and skilled enough to avoid the brunt of the Great Depression.

The lives of Earl "Lefty" Lewis and Herman E. Curtis and the situations described in *Bud, Not Buddy* are the exception, for the great majority of people suffered horribly during the period between 1929 and 1941. Parents often could not feed their children, so countless thousands of young people, some as young as eight years old, were abandoned or had to set out on their own in search of a meal and a warm place to sleep. These children survived the brutal life on the road by riding the rails, picking fruit, doing odd jobs, begging, stealing or whatever was necessary to get food.

Much of what I discovered about the depression I learned through research in books, which is a shame—I didn't take advantage of the family history that surrounded me for many years. I'm afraid that when I was younger and my grandparents and parents would start to talk about their lives during the depression, my eyes would glaze over and I'd think, "Oh, no, not those boring tall tales again!" and I'd find the most convenient excuse I could to get away from them. Now I feel a real sorrow when I think of all the knowledge, wisdom and stories that have been forever lost with the deaths of my grandparents.

Be smarter than I was: Go talk to Grandma and Grandpa, Mom and Dad and other relatives and friends. Discover and remember what they have to say about what they learned growing up. By keeping their stories alive you make them, and yourself, immortal.

# CONNECTIONS

# Royal Garden Blues

## Words and music by Clarence Williams and Spencer Williams

*A jazz classic, first recorded in 1921 by The Original Dixieland Jazz Band. The song has been performed by numerous jazz greats over the years, including Bix Beiderbecke and Louis Armstrong, and probably would have been performed by a real-life version of Herman E. Calloway's Dusky Devastators of the Depression.*

No use of talkin' no use of talkin'
You'll start in dog-walkin' no matter where.
There's jazz-copation blues modulation,
Just like a Haitian you'll rip and tear.
Most everybody likes the blues.

Here's why I'm ravin', here's why I'm ravin'
If it's blues you are cravin', just come on down.
You'll hear 'em playin', you'll hear 'em playin'
Soon you'll be sayin', "Hon, jazz me 'round,"
Because your feet they can't refuse.

What's that familiar strain
That true blue note refrain
It's drivin' me insane;
Can't keep still,
Though it's against my will;
I'm on my P's and Q's
I just can't refuse.

There goes that melody,
It sounds so good to me,
And I am up a tree;
It's a shame you don't know the name,
It's a brand new blues,
The Royal Garden Blues.

**Interlude:** Everybody grab somebody
And start jazzing 'round.

Hon, don't you hear that trombone moan?
Just listen to that saxophone.
Gee, hear that clarinet and flute,
Cornet jazzin' with a mute,
Makes me just throw myself away,
When I hear 'em play.

That weepin' melancholy strain,
Say, but it's soothing to the brain;
Just wanna get right up and dance,
Don't care I'll take most any chance;
No other blues I'd care to choose,
But Royal Garden Blues.

■  ■  ■

# *from* Mozart's Early Years
## Steve Boerner

*The Mozarts are one of history's most famous musical fami-
lies. They were also regular travelers, for Leopold Mozart,
a respected court composer and conductor from Salzburg,
Austria, lost no time in showing off to the world his son
Wolfgang's genius. At the age of six, Wolfgang was already
touring European capitals in the company of his parents
and his sister "Nannerl."*

### 'We are being talked of everywhere'

A few days later the Mozart family landed at Vienna's
Danube Canal pier, where Wolfgang speeded their passage
through customs by pulling out his fiddle and charming the
inspector with a minuet. All of Vienna, it seemed, was anx-
iously awaiting the arrival of the prodigies from Salzburg.
"We are already being talked of everywhere," Leopold
reported to Lorenz Hagenauer, his friend and landlord back
home. "Everyone is amazed, especially at the boy, and everyone whom I have heard says that his genius is incompre-
hensible." The children's appearance at Schönbrunn Palace
on October 13 was judged by Leopold to be a smashing
success. He wrote: "Their Majesties received us with such
extraordinary graciousness that, when I shall tell of it, people will declare that I have made it up. Suffice it to say that
[Wolfgang] jumped up on the Empress' lap, put his arms
round her neck and kissed her heartily."

### Taking society by storm

With that, the floodgates were opened and the invitations
poured in. Because each appearance was rewarded—the

∙∙∙∙∙∙∙∙∙∙∙∙∙∙∙∙∙∙∙∙∙∙∙∙∙∙∙∙∙∙∙∙∙∙∙∙∙∙∙∙∙∙∙∙∙∙∙∙∙∙

empress sent an honorarium of 100 ducats[1]—Leopold tried to arrange as many concerts as possible."Today we were at the French Ambassador's. Tomorrow we are invited to Count Harrach's from four to six, but which Count Harrach he is I do not know. I shall see where the carriage takes us to," Leopold wrote. "The nobles send us their invitations four, five, six to eight days in advance, in order not to miss us."

The pattern established here would be repeated in major centers all over Europe. First, Wolfgang and Nannerl[2] would perform at the most influential local court. Then private concerts would follow as the lesser nobility competed to entertain one another with an appearance by the "miracle children" of Salzburg. Payment came in the form of hard currency or gifts. When private concerts didn't pay the bills, the children would be put on public display. Public or private, the programs could last anywhere from one and a half to three hours. Two programs per day were the rule. "Reading those details of those days in Vienna," sighs biographer Erich Schenk, "we are inclined to say 'poor children.'"

In Leopold's defense, it should be noted that in his day (as in our own) it was not uncommon for child prodigies to be taken on tour. Leopold himself was convinced that it was God's will that he exhibit his children throughout Europe. That he did it with an eye toward his own future as well as that of his children . . . well, it was all the same to him, and to Anna Maria[3] and the children too. Never in their wildest dreams did any of them imagine that there would ever be a time when they would not be together. From start to finish, music was a family business.

---

1. Gold or silver coins then widely used in Europe.
2. Nannerl (a nickname for Anna Maria) usually played the harpsichord.
3. Wolfgang's mother.

## The price of success

Almost lost among Leopold's letters of this period is a brief reference to the fact that his son was cutting a new tooth. This otherwise mundane comment is a startling reminder of just how small he was . . . Wolfgang Mozart, the toast of Viennese society, was still two months shy of his seventh birthday.

The Mozarts departed Vienna on December 31 (in style, for Leopold had purchased a carriage) and arrived in Salzburg five days later. Wolfgang had fallen ill again, this time from acute rheumatoid arthritis, and spent his first week home in bed. By now, however, Leopold's appetite for travel was thoroughly whetted. In Vienna he had been invited to Versailles by the French ambassador. He decided to accept this offer and, with his sights firmly fixed upon France, departed with his family yet again from Salzburg on June 9. This time they would be gone for more than three years.

## The road to Paris

Eighteenth-century Europe, knit together by a dependable postal service and reliable roads, was becoming increasingly cosmopolitan. It wasn't at all unusual for professionals (such as musicians) to travel hundreds or even thousands of miles over the course of their careers. Even a middle-class, musical family could safely journey from Salzburg to Paris—and expect to make a profit by doing so.

Of course, *reliable* is a relative term when describing the roads of this period. In December, Leopold had complained of the frozen, rutted road between Pressburg and Vienna. The road to Wasserburg, at the very outset of his ambitious grand tour, shattered the wheel of the family's new carriage. Conditions inside the carriage—unheated and mounted on a crude suspension system that did little to soften the constant bumps and bangs—were anything but comfortable. Somehow the family endured it.

As an adult, Wolfgang would pass these hours on the road by composing. It was impossible to write—the jolting carriage would hardly allow that. But compose he would, carrying the music in his head until he had a chance to jot it down.

On this journey, a much younger Mozart let his imagination wander far beyond the cramped confines of the carriage. As the hours rolled by, he invented an imaginary land and named it the Kingdom of Back. "Why by this name, I can no longer recall," his sister wrote much later. "This kingdom and its inhabitants were endowed with everything that could make good and happy children out of them." Little Wolferl himself was the king of Back, and became so immersed in its administration that he persuaded Sebastian Winter, the family servant, to make a map of it and dictated to him the names of all the cities, villages and market towns.

## A visit to Versailles

Upon reaching Paris, Leopold wasted no time in making connections. One of his first acquaintances was Baron Friedrich Melchior Grimm, a German national who had resided in Paris since 1749. Grimm . . . arranged concerts at which Wolfgang and Nannerl performed, and also arranged the children's appearance at the French court.

Grimm became the family's best friend and most effective publicist. In his *Correspondance*, which circulated in handwritten manuscript to an elite group of subscribers throughout

Europe, he effusively praised the accomplishments and talents of Leopold's children: "His daughter, eleven years of age, plays the harpsichord in the most brilliant manner; she performs the longest and most difficult pieces with an astonishing precision. Her brother, who will be seven years old next February, is such an extraordinary phenomenon that one is hard put to it to believe what one sees with one's eyes and hears with one's ears."

On Christmas Eve the Mozarts moved to Versailles for two weeks, long enough to give them taste of life in that most famous of all European courts. Leopold was predictably pragmatic, mostly making note of how expensive everything was. But he had time for gossip too: "Madame de Pompadour[4] is still a handsome woman. . . . She is extremely haughty and still rules over everything."

The Marquise may have been distant and aloof, but that was not the case with Queen Maria Leszczynska[5] and Louis XV. The royal couple invited the Mozarts to court dinner on New Year's Day, and then insisted that the family stand behind them during the meal. "My Wolfgang was graciously privileged to stand beside the Queen the whole time, to talk constantly to her, entertain her and kiss her hands repeatedly, besides partaking of the dishes which she handed him from the table," Leopold wrote. "I stood beside him, and on the other side of the King . . . stood my wife and daughter."

■ ■ ■

4. Honorific name of Jeanne-Antoinette Poisson (1721–1764), influential patron of the arts and mistress of King Louis XV.
5. Queen of France (1703–1768), daughter of deposed King Stanislas of Poland.

# How the Great Depression Changed Detroit

**Jenny Nolan**
*The Detroit News*

*Detroit—"Motown," "Motor City"—is, of course, the center of U.S. automobile production and the largest city of Michigan, home state of Bud Caldwell and of his creator, Christopher Paul Curtis. It was also the most important American industrial center during the 1920s and '30s and as such particularly hard-hit by the Depression.*

Detroit produced more than 5,337,000 vehicles in 1929. The city had had a decade of prosperity. . . . The Detroit Zoo opened. The Detroit-Windsor Tunnel opened to autos under the Detroit River and the Ambassador Bridge above. Covered Wagon Co. of Detroit began manufacturing Covered Wagon trailer coaches (mobile homes). Mayor Charles Bowles was recalled by voters and Frank Murphy was elected.

On Tuesday, Oct. 29, [1929], the stock market crashed.

By 1930, car production was down to 3,363,000. In Detroit, Prohibition had been in effect for 10 years, but nightclubs thrived and gangs controlled the liquor trade. July was known as Bloody July after 10 were murdered by gangsters and radio commentator Jerry Buckley was killed in the lobby of the LaSalle Hotel.

Unemployment was becoming a huge problem: on Sept. 25, a list of Detroit registration places for the unemployed was announced. By the end of that day, 19,412 jobless had registered; 46,314 had registered by the 26th; by Sept. 29, just four days after the announcement, 75,704 had registered.

But poverty had not diminished moral rectitude: a man who had accepted a charitable donation of a shirt returned the diamond cufflinks he found in the cuffs.

The Mayor's Commission on Unemployment came up with the idea of the jobless becoming apple vendors. The idea came from a similar plan in New York City. Veterans and men with dependents were eligible. Apples were bought from Washington State growers directly at the produce terminal and sold for 5¢ each. Vendors had to pay for the first box, which was under two dollars. Vendors were licensed and had to be Detroiters with at least one year of residence, and were assigned to specific locations. Some 11,000 apples were sold the first day, November 24, 1930, by 150 vendors. Busy corners were rotated so that one man didn't have the best spot. At one time there were 700 apple vendors, but by 1934, they were on the wane with only 50 older men participating.

By 1931, the situation was critical. There were unemployment relief demonstrations in front of City Hall on Jan. 2. Auto production went down to 1,332,000 units. The idled Fisher plant became the City Municipal Lodging House, with heat, lights, showers and meals. But with the despair of joblessness came a corresponding increase in kindness.

Sen. James Couzens donated $200,000 and Louis Mendelsohn $100,000. Rosenberg's Department store

••••••••••••••••••••••••••••••••••••••••••••••

delivered 1,000 food baskets and Hudson's gave $10,000.
As many as 1,600 physicians donated free medical care
under the auspices of the Medical Relief Committee.

Thrift Gardens were planted in the spring of 1931.
Acreage was donated so that families could grow their own
food. There were 4,369 gardens the first year and 7,000 by
1933. Clothing drives were always in progress. They were
held by police, churches and schools. The Red Cross sent
1,200,000 yards of fabric here in Sept. 1932. The Red Wings[1]
had fans bring clothes to get into the game. Hudson Motor
Car Co. cutters cut out fabric for boys shirts. Country
parishes of the Archdiocese of Detroit donated surplus
crops to Detroit, which in Jan. 1931 was declared by the
U.S. Census to be the hardest hit of 19 cities, followed
by Cleveland, Chicago, Buffalo and Philadelphia.

In 1932, some landlords had been allowing families
to live rent free for months, counting on a promise by the
Welfare Department that they would start to be paid in July.
When the department announced in July that no money
would be forthcoming, Clark Park was set up as an emergency camp for evicted families. Private citizens and the
National Guard donated tents. The women had sewing
circles, the children used the playgrounds and the men
looked for work. Neighbors who initially opposed the
encampment ended up donating food and organizing
games for the children.

On March 7, the Ford Hunger March from Detroit
was organized by John Schmies, communist candidate for
mayor of Detroit, and led by Albert Goetz. Three thousand

1. Local ice hockey team.

marched from Detroit to Dearborn asking for union recognition, full employment (Ford had had massive layoffs) and a six hour work day with no reduction in wages. When Dearborn police attempted to stop them at the [city limits], rioting resulted. Four marchers were killed and hundreds were injured. About 15,000 marched in the funeral procession, and 30,000 gathered at the grave to hear the communist workers' anthem, "The International."

Tax delinquencies caused a fiscal crisis in Detroit. City employee salaries were reduced and welfare was sharply reduced. Doctors gave free care to 4,000 and the Fisher plant, 'Fisher Lodge' which had been closed, reopened to homeless men.

On March 31, Roosevelt signed the Civil Conservation Corps into law. On April 19, he took the nation off the gold standard. On April 7, beer and wine were legalized. On Nov. 17, the United States recognized the Soviet government. On Oct. 14, Germany withdrew from the League of Nations[2]. On Dec. 5, Repeal was ratified[3]; it took effect in Michigan Dec. 30.

The Civil Conservation Corps was a government program that was considered a resounding success. Young men lived in camps and did forestry work. Michigan provided many of the workers as well as receiving many of the benefits of the program. The Camps were run by military men, mostly reserve army officers. The first applicants in Michigan were

2. Organization based in Geneva, Switzerland. The League was a precursor to the United Nations, but was almost completely ineffective. The United States never joined.

3. Repeal of the Eighteenth Amendment to the Constitution, which had imposed Prohibition, a nationwide ban on alcoholic drinks, in 1919.

taken April 10, 1933. The age span was 18 to 25, along with
some World War I veterans. Participants made $30 a month,
with $22 to $25 sent home to their families. Within 16 months,
there were 61 camps in Michigan. They wore blue denim
uniforms and were initially referred to derogatorily as 'wood.'
In the first year in Michigan, they planted 28,000,000 trees
and cleared 2,491 miles of truck trails. Eventually, they reduced fire hazards, reduced losses from tree diseases, built
13 lookout houses, 14 lookout towers, cleared 1,000 acres
for campgrounds, built 4,000 fire towers, strung 75,000 miles
of telephone wire, built 132,000 miles of road, fought fires,
dyked flooding river banks and planted 1,800,000,000 trees.
They put in 8-hour days and schooling was available. And
the program was credited with reducing the prison popula-
tion, by giving young men something to do and by straighten-
ing them out.

In 1934, Prohibition was over and the cult of lawless-
ness was waning. John Dillinger, Clyde Barrow and Bonnie
Parker and Pretty Boy Floyd[4] were all killed by lawmen.
Billy Sunday opened his second revival in Detroit.

In 1935, Detroit became the City of Champions: The
Tigers won the World Series against the Cubs, the Lions
won the NFL championship and the Red Wings won the
Stanley Cup. Gar Wood with his racing boats and Olympic
track star Eddie "the Midnight Express" Tolan were already
champs and Joe Louis was to become the heavyweight
champion in 1937.

By the late 1930s, Hitler had annexed Austria. He was
ceded part of Czechoslovakia and invaded the rest. Italy

---

4. Notorious gangsters of the period.

occupied Albania and Ethiopia. As Europe marched toward war, the United States geared up to build the tanks and planes to fight it. Factories began to hire again, and men went back to work and eventually off to war.

Detroit had struggled through the Great Depression with ingenuity, generosity, pride and grit.

**Copyright 2000** *The Detroit News*

■  ■  ■

# *from* Black Boy
## Richard Wright

*Richard Wright (1908–1960) was one of the preeminent American novelists of his age.* Black Boy *is a harrowing account of his impoverished childhood and youth. In this scene his mother, while not dead, essentially departs his everyday life and fills him with determination to confront life in a new and different way.*

I was glad to see my mother. She was much better, though still abed. Another operation had been advised by the doctor and there was hope for recovery. But I was anxious. Why another operation? A victim myself of too many hopes that had never led anywhere, I was for letting my mother remain as she was. My feelings were governed by fear and I spoke to no one about them. I had already begun to sense that my feelings varied too far from those of the people around me for me to blab about what I felt.

I did not re-enter school. Instead, I played alone in the back yard, bouncing a rubber ball off the fence, drawing figures in the soft clay with an old knife, or reading what books I found about the house. I ached to be of an age to take care of myself.

Uncle Edward arrived . . . to take my mother to Clarksdale for the operation; at the last moment I insisted upon being taken with them. I dressed hurriedly and we went to the station. Throughout the journey I sat brooding, afraid to look at my mother, wanting to return home and yet wanting to go on. We reached Clarksdale and hired a taxi to the doctor's office. My mother was jolly, brave, smiling, but but I knew that she was as doubtful as I was. When we reached the doctor's waiting room the conviction settled in me that my mother would never be well again. Finally the doctor came out in his white coat and shook hands with me, then took my mother inside. Uncle Edward left to make arrangements for a room and a nurse. I felt crushed. I waited. Hours later the doctor came to the door.

"How's my mother?"

"Fine!" he said.

"Will she be all right?"

"Everything'll clear up in a few days."

"Can I see her now?"

"No, not now."

Later Uncle Edward returned with an ambulance and two men who carried a stretcher. They entered the doctor's office and brought out my mother; she lay with closed eyes, her body swathed in white. I wanted to run to the stretcher and touch her, but I could not move.

"Why are they taking mama that way?" I asked Uncle Edward.

"There are no hospital facilities for colored, and this is the way we have to do it," he said.

I watched the men take the stretcher down the steps; then I stood on the sidewalk and watched them lift my mother into the ambulance and drive away. I knew that my mother had gone out of my life; I could feel it.

Uncle Edward and I stayed at a boardinghouse; each morning he went to . . . inquire about my mother and each time he returned gloomy and silent. Finally he told me that he was taking my mother back home.

"What chance has mama, really?" I asked him.

"She's very sick," he said.

We left Clarksdale; my mother rode on a stretcher in the baggage car with Uncle Edward attending her. Back home, she lay for days, groaning, her eyes vacant. Doctors visited her and left without any comment. Granny grew frantic. Uncle Edward, who had gone home, returned and still more doctors were called in. They told us that a blood clot had formed on my mother's brain and that another paralytic stroke had set in.

Once, in the night, my mother called me to her bed and told me that she could not endure the pain, that she wanted to die. I held her hand and begged her to be quiet. That night I ceased to react to my mother; my feelings were frozen. I merely waited upon her, knowing that she was suffering. She remained abed ten years, gradually growing better, but never completely recovering, relapsing periodically into her paralytic state. The family had stripped itself of money to fight my mother's illness and there was no more forthcoming. Her illness gradually became an accepted thing in the house, something that could not be stopped or helped.

My mother's suffering grew into a symbol in my mind, gathering to itself all the poverty, the ignorance, the helplessness; the painful, baffling, hunger-ridden days and hours; the restless moving, the futile seeking, the uncertainty, the fear, the dread; the meaningless pain and the endless suffering. Her life set the emotional tone of my life, colored the men and women I was to meet in the future, conditioned my relation to events that had not yet happened, determined my attitude to situations and circumstances I had yet to face. A somberness of spirit that I was never to lose settled over me during the slow years of my mother's unrelieved suffering, a somberness that was to make me stand apart and look upon excessive joy with suspicion, that was to make me self-conscious, that was to make me keep forever on the move, as though to escape a nameless fate seeking to overtake me.

At the age of twelve, before I had had one full year of formal schooling, I had a conception of life that no experience would ever erase, a predilection for what was real that no argument could ever gainsay, a sense of the world that was mine and mine alone, a notion as to what life meant that no education could ever alter, a conviction that the meaning of living came only when one was struggling to wring a meaning out of meaningless suffering.

At the age of twelve I had an attitude toward life that was to endure, that was to make me seek those areas of living that would keep it alive, that was to make me skeptical of everything while seeking everything, tolerant of all and yet critical. The spirit I had caught gave me insight into the sufferings of others, made me gravitate toward those whose feelings were like my own, made me sit for hours while others told me of their lives, made me strangely tender and cruel, violent and peaceful.

It made me want to drive coldly to the heart of every question and lay it open to the core of suffering I knew I would find there. It made me love burrowing into psychology, into realistic and naturalistic fiction and art, into those whirlpools of politics that had the power to claim the whole of men's souls. It directed my loyalties to the side of men in rebellion; it made me love talk that sought answers to questions that could help nobody, that could only keep alive in me that enthralling sense of wonder and awe in the face of the drama of human feeling which is hidden by the external drama of life.

■   ■   ■

# The Life of A. Philip Randolph
## Kate Tuttle

*"Lefty" Lewis, in* Bud, Not Buddy, *tells Bud about union-organizing activities in Grand Rapids involving the Pullman porters. It is doubtful whether any such activities in the 1930s would have been successful without the leadership of A. Philip Randolph.*

Although many civil rights leaders focused on voting, education, and other governmental functions, [Asa] Philip Randolph spent his long career as a labor leader working to bring more and better jobs to African Americans. After a long, successful battle to win representation for the nation's Pullman porters, Randolph was instrumental in the formation of the Fair Employment Practices Commission (FEPC), which protected African Americans against job discrimination in the army and defense industries. In addition, Randolph cofounded and edited socialist black magazine *The Messenger.*

The son of a minister, Randolph grew up in Jacksonville, Florida and graduated from the Cookman Institute in 1907. A lack of economic opportunity for blacks led Randolph, the class valedictorian, into a series of menial jobs until 1911, when he moved to New York City. Working as an elevator operator and living in Harlem, Randolph took classes at the City College of New York and New York University, acted in amateur theatricals, and eventually took a job with a Harlem employment agency.

In 1914 Randolph met Chandler Owen, whose progressive politics and interest in socialism matched his own. In 1917 the two founded *The Messenger,* whose editorials strongly opposed U.S. entry into World War I, saying that "no intelligent Negro is willing to lay down his life for the United States as it now exists." Though the magazine was never profitable, it was influential, offering a more radical voice than that of W. E. B. Du Bois's *The Crisis* or the even more conventional *New York Age. The Messenger*, with its advocacy of labor unions, was especially popular among Pullman porters, all of whom were black, who served white railroad passengers in luxurious sleeping cars. Founded just after the Civil War, the Pullman company had by the 1920s become the nation's single largest employer of African Americans. Many of the Pullman porters were college graduates who enjoyed great respect within their communities, but at work they were subjected to unfair and discriminatory practices.

In 1925, with Randolph at the helm, the Brotherhood of Sleeping Car Porters (BSCP) began organizing the nearly 10,000 porters. For ten years, Randolph kept the members unified and inspired, often in the face of intimidation and firings, while he negotiated with the president and Congress to amend the Railway Labor Act. Finally, in a hard-won victory hailed by African Americans and progressives nationwide, the company recognized their union in 1935.

Randolph continued to fight for racial and economic justice in the late 1930s as president of the National Negro Congress before resigning in protest over its increasing domination by Communists. In 1940 he returned to the issue of jobs, joining National Association for the Advancement of Colored People (NAACP) secretary Walter White and T. Arnold Hill of the National Urban League in urging President Franklin D. Roosevelt to desegregate the military and defense industries before World War II. After an unsatisfactory resolution to a meeting with the president, Randolph began planning a march on Washington, D.C., by the BSCP and others to demand "the right to work and fight for our country." The date for at least 10,000 African Americans to demonstrate before the Lincoln Memorial was set for July 1, 1941. Despite the President's wish to avoid a mass demonstration, Randolph refused to call off the march unless Roosevelt banned discrimination in the burgeoning defense industries. Following another meeting with Randolph and White, the president at last issued Executive Order 8002, which not only outlawed such discrimination but also established the Fair Employment Practices Committee (FEPC) to investigate breaches of the order.

Though the FEPC operated only from 1941 to 1946, Randolph continued to push for his other goal: desegregation of the U.S. armed forces. When President Harry S. Truman instituted a peacetime draft, Randolph told him "this time Negroes will not take a Jim Crow draft lying down." In July 1948 Truman signed Executive Order 9981, finally ending the historic segregation of African American soldiers.

Throughout the 1950s, Randolph worked with the NAACP and other civil rights leaders. He helped plan and spoke at "Pilgrimage Day," a 1957 prayer meeting in Washington, D.C. He met with President Dwight D. Eisenhower to push for faster school integration in the wake of *Brown* v. *Board of Education* and planned a 1958 Youth March for Integrated Schools. He also continued his union work, and became vice president of the newly consolidated AFL-CIO from 1955 to 1968.

Randolph's brainchild, the March on Washington Movement, bore new fruit in 1963 with the help of Bayard Rustin and the Rev. Martin Luther King Jr., who, along with Randolph, mobilized the largest demonstration of the Civil Rights Movement. Speaking before King, the 74-year-old

Randolph exhorted the crowd of 250,000 to take part in a "revolution for jobs and freedom." The next year, President Lyndon B. Johnson signed the Civil Rights Act of 1964 and awarded Randolph the Presidential Medal of Freedom. In his final years, Randolph established the A. Philip Randolph Institute, a job skills and training bureau in Harlem. Upon Randolph's death in 1979, Rustin said of his late colleague, "No individual did more to help the poor, the dispossessed and the working class . . . than A. Philip Randolph."

■　■　■

# An Hour with Abuelo
## Judith Ortiz Cofer

*Like Bud Caldwell, Arturo is having problems relating to his grandfather, and like Bud he has to overcome some prejudices and misconceptions of his own in order to bridge the generation gap.*

"Just one hour, *una hora,* is all I'm asking of you, son." My grandfather is in a nursing home in Brooklyn, and my mother wants me to spend some time with him, since the doctors say that he doesn't have too long to go now. I don't have much time left on my summer vacation, and there's a stack of books next to my bed I've got to read if I'm going to get into the AP English class I want. I'm going stupid in some of my classes, and Mr. Williams, the principal at Central, said that if I passed some reading tests, he'd let me move up.

Besides, I hate the place, the old people's home, especially the way it smells like industrial-strength ammonia and other stuff I won't mention, since it turns my stomach. And really the abuelo always has a lot of relatives visiting him, so I've gotten out of going out there except at Christmas, when a whole van-load of grandchildren are herded over there to give him gifts and a hug. We all make it quick and spend the rest of the time in the recreation area, where they play checkers and stuff with some of the old people's games, and I catch up on back issues of *Modern Maturity.* I'm not picky, I'll read almost anything.

Anyway, after my mother nags me for about a week, I let her drive me to Golden Years. She drops me off in front. She wants me to go in alone and have a "good time" talking to Abuelo. I tell her to be back in one hour or I'll take the bus back to Paterson. She squeezes my hand and says, *"Gracias, hijo,"* in a choked-up voice like I'm doing her a big favor.

I get depressed the minute I walk into the place. They line up the old people in wheelchairs in the hallway as if they were about to be raced to the finish line by orderlies who don't even look at them when they push them here and there. I walk fast to room 10, Abuelo's "suite." He is sitting up in his bed writing with a pencil in one of those old-fashioned black hardback notebooks. It has the outline of the island of Puerto Rico on it. I slide into the hard vinyl chair by his bed. He sort of smiles and the lines on his face get deeper, but he doesn't say anything. Since I'm supposed to talk to him, I say, "What are you doing, Abuelo, writing the story of your life?"

It's supposed to be a joke, but he answers, "Sí, how did you know, Arturo?"

His name is Arturo too. I was named after him. I don't really know my grandfather. His children, including my mother came to New York and New Jersey (where I was born) and he stayed on the Island until my grandmother died. Then he got sick, and since nobody could leave their jobs to go take care of him, they brought him to this nursing home in Brooklyn. I see him a couple of times a year, but he's always surrounded by his sons and daughters. My mother tells me that Don Arturo had once been a teacher back in Puerto Rico, but had lost his job after the war. Then he became a farmer. She's always saying in a sad voice, "Ay, bendito! What a waste of a fine mind." Then she usually shrugs her shoulders and says, *"Así es la vida."* That's the way life is. It sometimes makes me mad that the adults

I know just accept whatever is thrown at them because "that's the way things are." Not for me. I go after what I want.

Anyway, Abuelo is looking at me like he was trying to see into my head, but he doesn't say anything. Since I like stories, I decide I may as well ask him if he'll read me what he wrote.

I look at my watch: I've already used up twenty minutes of the hour I promised my mother.

Abuelo starts talking in his slow way. He speaks what my mother calls book English. He taught himself from the dictionary, and his words sound stiff, like he's sounding them out in his head before he says them. With his children he speaks Spanish, and that funny book English with us grandchildren. I'm surprised that he's still so sharp, because his body is shrinking like a crumpled-up brown paper sack with some bones in it. But I can see from looking into his eyes that the light is still on in there.

"It is a short story, Arturo. The story of my life. It will not take very much time to read it."

"I have time, Abuelo." I'm a little embarrassed that he saw me looking at my watch.

"Yes, hijo. You have spoken the truth. La verdad. You have much time."

Abuelo reads: " 'I loved words from the beginning of my life. In the *campo* where I was born one of seven sons, there were few books. My mother read them to us over and over: the Bible, the stories of Spanish conquistadors and of pirates that she had read as a child and brought with her from the city of Mayagüez; that was before she married my father, a coffee bean farmer; and she taught us words from the newspaper that a boy on a horse brought every week to her. She taught each of us how to write on a slate with chalks that she ordered by mail every year. We used those chalks until they were so small that you lost them between your fingers.

"'I always wanted to be a writer and a teacher. With my heart and my soul I knew that I wanted to be around books all of my life. And so against the wishes of my father, who wanted all his sons to help him on the land, she sent me to high school in Mayagüez. For four years I boarded with a couple she knew. I paid my rent in labor, and I ate vegetables I grew myself. I wore my clothes until they were thin as parchment. But I graduated at the top of my class! My whole family came to see me that day. My mother brought me a beautiful *guayabera,* a white shirt made of the finest cotton and embroidered by her own hands. I was a happy young man.

"'In those days you could teach in a country school with a high school diploma. So I went back to my mountain village and got a job teaching all grades in a little classroom built by the parents of my students.

"'I had books sent to me by the government. I felt like a rich man although the pay was very small. I had books. All the books I wanted! I taught my students how to read poetry and plays, and how to write them. We made up songs and put on shows for the parents. It was a beautiful time for me.

"'Then the war came, and the American President said that all Puerto Rican men would be drafted. I wrote to our governor and explained that I was the only teacher in the mountain village. I told him that the children would go back to the fields and grow up ignorant if I could not teach them their letters. I said that I thought I was a better teacher than a soldier. The governor did not answer my letter. I went into the U.S. Army.

"'I told my sergeant that I could be a teacher in the army. I could teach all the farm boys their letters so that they could read the instructions on the ammunition boxes and not blow themselves up. The sergeant said I was too smart for my own good, and gave me a job cleaning latrines. He said to me there is reading material for you there, scholar. Read the writing on the walls. I spent the war mopping floors and cleaning toilets.

"'When I came back to the Island, things had changed. You had to have a college degree to teach school, even the lower grades. My parents were sick, two of my brothers had been killed in the war, the others had stayed in Nueva York. I was the only one left to help the old people. I became a farmer. I married a good woman who gave me many good children. I taught them all how to read and write before they started school.'"

Abuelo then puts the notebook down on his lap and closes his eyes.

"*Así es la vida* is the title of my book," he says in a whisper, almost to himself. Maybe he's forgotten that I'm there.

For a long time he doesn't say anything else. I think that he's sleeping, but then I see that he's watching me through half-closed lids, maybe waiting for my opinion of his writing. I'm trying to think of something nice to say. I liked it all, but not the title. And I think that he could've been a teacher if he had wanted to bad enough. Nobody is going to stop me from doing what I want with my life. I'm not going to let la vida get in my way. I want to discuss this with him, but the words are not coming into my head in Spanish just yet. I'm about to ask him why he didn't keep fighting to make his dream come true, when an old lady in hot-pink running shoes sort of appears at the door.

She is wearing a pink jogging outfit too. The world's oldest marathoner, I say to myself. She calls out to my grandfather in a flirty voice, "Yoo-hoo, Arturo, remember what day this is? It's poetry-reading day in the rec room! you promised us you'd read your new one today."

I see my abuelo perking up almost immediately. He points to his wheelchair, which is hanging like a huge metal bat in the open closet. He makes it obvious that he wants me to get it. I put it together, and with Mrs. Pink Running Shoes's help, we get him in it. Then he says in a strong deep voice I hardly recognize, "Arturo, get that notebook from the table please."

I hand him another map-of-the-Island notebook—this one is red. On it in big letters it says, *POEMAS DE ARTURO.*

I start to push him toward the rec room, but he shakes his finger at me.

"Arturo, look at your watch now. I believe your time is over." He gives me a wicked smile.

Then with her pushing the wheelchair—maybe a little too fast—they roll down the hall. He is already reading from his notebook, and she's making bird noises. I look at my watch and the hour is up, to the minute. I can't help but think that my abuelo has been timing *me.* He cracks me up. I walk slowly down the hall toward the exit sign. I want my mother to have to wait a little. I don't want her to think that I'm in a hurry or anything.

■    ■    ■

# Christopher Paul Curtis
## (1953–   )

Christopher Paul Curtis is the author of *The Watsons Go to Birmingham—1963,* one of the most highly acclaimed first novels for young readers in recent years. It was singled out for many awards, among them a Newbery Honor and a Coretta Scott King Honor, and has been a bestseller in hardcover and paperback.

Christopher Paul Curtis grew up in Flint, Michigan. After high school he began working on the assembly line at the Fisher Body Flint Plant No. 1 while attending the Flint branch of the University of Michigan. He is now a full-time writer. He and his wife, Kay, have two children, Steven and Cydney. The Curtis family lives in Windsor, Ontario, Canada.

■   ■   ■